For Better or For Worse
A Blessing or A Curse?

Domestic Violence in the Christian Home

by

Melissa Martin

ACW Press
5501 N. 7th Ave. #502
Phoenix, AZ 85013

For Better or For Worse: A Blessing or A Curse?
Copyright © 1999
Melissa Martin
All rights reserved.

Cover design by Eric Walljasper

All rights reserved. No part of this book may be reproduced in whole or in part without written permission from the author, except by a reviewer who may quote brief passages in a review; nor may any part of this book be reproduced, stored in a retrieval system, or transmitted in any form or by any means electronic, mechanical, including photocopying, recording, or other, without permission in writing from the author, except as provided by USA copyright law.

Unless otherwise noted, all Scripture quotations are from *The New American Standard Bible*, © 1960, 1962, 1963, 1968, 1971, 1972, 1975, 1977 by the Lockman Foundation. Used by permission.

Scripture quotations marked NIV are taken from the *Holy Bible*, New International Version, copyright © 1973, 1978, 1984 by International Bible Society. Used by permission of Zondervan Publishing House. All rights reserved.

Scripture quotations marked KJV are from the *Holy Bible*, King James Version.

Scripture quotations marked LB are taken from The Living Bible, © 1971 owned by assignment by KNT Charitable Trust. All rights reserved.

Scripture quotations marked NLT are taken from the *Holy Bible*, New Living Translation, © 1996. Used by permission of Tyndale House Publishers, Inc., Wheaton, Illinois 60189. All rights reserved.

Publisher's Cataloging-in-Publication
(Provided by Quality Books, Inc.)

Martin, Melissa, 1959-
    For better or for worse : a blessing or a curse? :
domestic violence in the Christian home / by Melissa Martin
— 1st ed.
    p. cm.
    Includes bibliographical references and index.
    ISBN: 1-89-252504-6

1. Family violence--United States. 2. Family violence--Religious aspects--Christianity 3. Wife abuse--United Sates. 4. Wife abuse--Religious aspects--Christianity. 5. Church work with abused women --United States.   I. Title

HV6626.2.M37 1999   362.82'92'0973
                       QBI98-1470

Printed in the United States of America

To obtain more copies please contact:
Melissa Martin
P.O. Box 61
Circleville, OH 43113
See the order form in the back of this book.

Dedication

*This resource manual is dedicated to
Jehovah Rapha, Our God of Healing
and
to all His precious daughters and children in heaven
and on earth who have suffered, died from, or survived
domestic violence in their Christian homes.*

**The Lord is a refuge for the oppressed,
a stronghold in times of trouble.
Those who know your name will trust in you,
for you, Lord, have never forsaken those who seek you.
Psalm 9:9-10**

About the Author

Melissa Martin is a survivor of domestic violence. She is a Licensed Professional Clinical Counselor and a Licensed Social Worker in the state of Ohio with a Master of Arts Degree in Mental Health Counseling. Melissa is a Licensed Christian Counselor and Ordained Minister. She has over 10 years of experience working with abused women and children.

Contents

Preface 6
Acknowledgments 7
Who is This Resource Guide For? 8
Introduction 9
Chapter 1: Types of Abuse 11
Chapter 2: Crisis Intervention 21
Chapter 3: Christian Men Who Batter 51
Chapter 4: Women, Men, and The Bible 59
Chapter 5: Jesus Therapy 69
Chapter 6: Batterer to Believer 103
Chapter 7: Victim to Victor 115
Chapter 8: Trauma to Triumph 133
Chapter 9: Hurting To Hope 145
Chapter 10: Marital Restoration 155
Chapter 11: Prevention of Domestic Violence 167
Chapter 12: Poetry Therapy 175
Chapter 13: Tools for Change 187

Appendix A: Directory of Resources
National Domestic Violence Hotline 207
Domestic Violence Directory for Ohio (1998) 208
Domestic Violence Coalitions in the United States 211
National Religious Organizations Against Domestic Violence ... 215
National Organizations Against Domestic Violence 217
Information About Treatment Programs and Resources
    for Male Batterers 219
Treatment Programs: Male Support Groups 220
Christian Counseling Resources 222
National Religious AIDS 223
Organizations and Hotlines 223
National Pregnancy Help Resources 224
State Child Support Enforcement Offices 225
National Crisis Hotlines for Teenagers 226

Appendix B: Resources
Religious Resources 227
Video List on Domestic Violence 231
Resources for Teenagers 232
Resources for Children 233
Internet Addresses 235
Glossary 237
End Notes 239
Review of Chapters 242
Index 245
ABC's of Salvation 246

Preface

To the Lord Jesus Christ, Whom I serve, I offer my heartfelt thanks, for He has given me the privilege of writing this resource guide. During the last year while writing this publication, I have prayed fervently that my written words would bring hope and healing to victims, batterers, and their families. I have prayed that the words the Holy Spirit put upon my heart and pen would not offend one pastor, counselor, educator, helper, victim or batterer. The attacks of Satan have been mighty as I wrote. Satan wants to destroy God's families; but there is victory in the name of Jesus! Many are working to prevent domestic violence in the secular population. Resources, studies, and statistics are plentiful. I applaud these diligent workers. My purpose is to address domestic violence in the Christian population. Studies and statistics are scarce. It is not my intention to bring criticism upon the Christian community. My motives are pure. If but one life is saved from a premature death due to domestic violence, or but one family restored, then my written words are not in vain.

In His Service,

Melissa Martin

> ...And He said, "Write, for these
> words are faithful and true."
> **Revelation 21:5**

Acknowledgments

Thank you to the victims, survivors, and batterers who have graciously shared their stories so others may heal. All names have been changed for privacy and protection.

Who is This Resource Guide For?

Recognizing the seriousness of domestic violence in Christian families, this resource guide is addressed to several audiences:

- To wives who are victims of violence and desperately need the help of their church families.
- To husbands who are abusers and desperately need to be held accountable so healing restoration can begin.
- To pastors' wives who are afraid to tell the secret of violence in their homes.
- To pastors and religious leaders who are abusing their wives and need to confess the sin of domestic violence.
- To clergy, rabbis, and priests, for the purpose of educating every denomination, in every church, in every community in America. Domestic violence can appear in any congregation.
- To youth pastors and leaders whose teenagers may be involved in dating violence.
- To church congregations and laity. Church is a place to worship Almighty God; but church is also a spiritual hospital for the women, men, and children who are victims of family violence.
- To men, because the field of domestic violence is in need of men who will stand together to send a message to batterers. Real men do not beat their wives and children.
- To counselors and mental health professionals, so they may understand the dynamics of abuse in God's broken families.
- To educators, so they may teach and provide knowledge to break the cycle of generational domestic violence; and to students at seminaries and religious universities.
- To friends, parents, relatives, and helpers whose loved ones are suffering in violent relationships, and they do not know what to do.
- To secular agencies and domestic violence shelters, to help them learn about using the victims' faith as a source for healing and restoration.
- To police officers, attorneys, judges, and the court system, so they may better understand women of faith.

Introduction

It is estimated that one million Christian women are victimized by their husbands each year in America.[1] How does God view domestic violence? Love your neighbor as yourself—but not your wife. Domestic violence is a learned behavior; therefore, it can be unlearned. Domestic violence in the United States of America is a crime punishable by incarceration. It is against the law to abuse your wife! It is against God's law to abuse your wife! America, we have no choice but to look at the ugly secret of family violence. Christians, we have no choice but to look at domestic violence in homes of Christians, but we must admit the problem first. God's families are in crisis!

This resource guide is not intended to point fingers of blame. Its intent is to expose the secret of domestic violence, so healing can begin. This guide deals with women who are victims of domestic violence, because statistics show us that ninety-five percent of the victims are women.[2] The other victims are the children—children who will grow up and model the violent behaviors of their parents, so the cycle of violence will continue. The indirect victims are family, relatives, and friends who lose loved ones to violent deaths or stand helplessly by and listen to the loud silence of hidden violence.

Dear readers, please do not say, "I'm glad my church does not have any of those kinds of families." Domestic violence crosses all religious, racial, social, and economic borders. We must unite to address the issue of domestic violence in our Christian homes. I believe all Christians can work side-by-side to stop the violence and minister to God's broken families. We have the same goal—restoration of God's families!

Chapter One

Types of Abuse

What is the definition of domestic violence?
Battering is the establishment of control and fear in a relationship through violence and other forms of abuse. The batterer uses acts of violence and a series of behaviors, including intimidation, threats, psychological abuse, isolation, etc., to coerce and to control the other person. The violence may not happen often, but it remains as a hidden (and constant) terrorizing factor. (Uniform Crime Reports, Federal Bureau of Investigation, 1990)

Domestic violence is the threat, attempt, or act of physical harm made against you or a member of your family by another member or your family or someone you live with, or have lived with in the past as if you are related by blood or marriage. (Ross County Family Violence Council, 1995)

Domestic violence crosses all social, cultural, racial, ethnic, religious, and economic groups, as well as all ages and sexual identities. Domestic violence is a global issue, also.

The words "domestic violence" and "family violence" are interchangeable, and refer to violence among any members of a family. The words "marital violence" and "spousal battery" are also interchangeable, and refer to violence between husband and wife. "Partner violence" refers to husband and wife or unmarried singles.

Types of abuse
The eight types of abuse listed below are used by batterers to gain power and control over their wives and children. The abuse is on a continuum of mild to severe, with battering ranging in degree from verbal abuse on one end of the scale to physical abuse and even death on the other end. Physical abuse can of course be more readily measured, by the evidence of bruises, scars, and broken bones; but other types of abuse, while not visible, can be equally serious, leading to depression, post-traumatic stress disorder, and even suicide. All abuse is hurtful and harmful.

1. Physical
2. Emotional/psychological
3. Spiritual
4. Verbal
5. Sexual
6. Social
7. Economic/financial
8. Parental authority

Physical abuse in a Christian home

Physical violence is categorizes at different levels, according to intensity:

LEVEL 1	LEVEL 2	LEVEL 3	LEVEL 4
• shaking	• slapping	• punching	• using weapons to beat or cut her
• pushing	• pinching	• kicking	• breaking bones and choking
• twisting arm	• pulling hair	• throwing her	• knocking out teeth
• restraining	• bruising	• biting	• burning with cigarettes

What constitutes physical abuse? Is it one slap, one push, or one kick? Is it black eyes and bruises? Is it bloodied lips and broken bones? Is it the pulling of hair or a knocked-out tooth? Is it choking or biting? Is it forcible marital rape? Is it the refusal of medical treatment and/or medicine? Is it being threatened with destructive acts, such as punching walls, breaking her possessions, throwing household items, or killing family pets?

All of these violent acts are physical abuse. At what point should wives seek help? A wife should seek help after the very first act of abuse, before it escalates. At what point in the marriage is the physical violence enough that a woman should leave temporarily? For ministers, addressing physical violence in a Christian marriage creates a dilemma if the husband will neither stop the physical abuse nor accept help. Ministers are in the business of keeping families together, but not at the cost of lives.

Did Adam batter Eve? Did Abraham batter Sarah? Did Moses batter Zipporah? Did Jacob batter Rachel? Did Isaac batter Rebekah? Did Joseph batter Mary? Not in the Bible. There is no record of these men battering their wives. There are no scripture verses that advocate violence in marriage.

Temporary separation is a solution, if the abuser will not stop the physical violence and accept help. God is in the business of keeping families together, but the wives and children MUST be safe and protected during the period of counseling, healing, and restoration. Healing cannot take place until the physical abuse stops. Fortunately, we serve a God of forgiveness. While teaching in the Ohio prison system, I have had the opportunity to talk with inmates who are incarcerated for domestic violence. Through Jesus, counseling, and education about the causes of violence, they have unlearned their violent behavior and changed their ways.

In 1995, the National Domestic Violence Project provided reconstructive surgery for 500 battered women free of charge. These were women beaten by their husbands or partners.[1] As abused women age, they may develop arthritis from past physical abuse. Many suffer permanent damage to their bodies: blindness, hearing loss, etc. The long-term effects of domestic violence are many, and not yet fully documented.

Emotional/psychological abuse

- blaming
- ridicule
- neglecting physical needs
- committing adultery
- minimizes injuries

- isolation from others
- criticism
- abuse of pets
- constant phone calls
- male superiority

- ignoring her
- criticizing family, friends
- makes threats to kill
- monitoring conversations
- entitlement to control

The physical abuse is accompanied by emotional abuse. The wife is a prisoner in her own home. She must give an account of how each hour in her day is spent—every day. He may check the mileage on the car to see if she has disobeyed by driving, or remove a vital car component. He may forbid her to obtain or renew her driver's license. She is allowed only minimal contact with family and friends. She must listen to his raging jealousy and unfounded accusations of extra-marital affairs. She is degraded and humiliated. His weapons are oppression and intimidation. He uses threats and ridicules her. He is a master of "mind games" and manipulation, a master at "slavery of the mind." He is a pathological liar. He seeks to control her mind, body, soul, and spirit.

He gives her the silent treatment to punish her, which can last for days or even weeks. He is charming in public and brutal in private. Adultery by the husband, whether overt or covert, is emotional abuse as well as spiritual abuse. Trust is broken, and the scars are deep.

The majority of the battered women I counsel suffer from severe depression caused by years of physical, emotional, verbal, social, and spiritual abuse. By the time help is sought, some women are suicidal. The only reason they do not kill themselves is love for their children and Jesus. A few women turn to alcohol and/or drugs; prescription or nonprescription, to escape their twin realities of fear and pain.

Spiritual abuse

If a woman in your church experiences any of the following, she is suffering spiritual abuse:
- She is not allowed to pay tithes or offerings to the church.
- She is not allowed to teach their children about the Bible. Her husband may even tell the children that there is no God and refuse to attend church services.
- She is falsely accused of having an affair with the pastor, a deacon, or church member. Her husband often attends church and abuses her at home.
- She is not allowed to read her Bible or keep it in the home.
- He may command her to read nothing but the Bible and never miss any church services.
- He may refuse to pray or read the Bible with her because of her gender.
- He may spend time ministering to other people, yet neglect his own family.
- He may give so much of their income (beyond tithing) to the church that his wife's and children's basic needs are not met.

The batterer uses the Bible as a weapon, misusing Scripture verses to control, dominate, and manipulate. Daily shouting ensures his wife's submission. This husband is not a spiritual leader; he is a spiritual tyrant. In Genesis 1:28, God gave dominion to both man and woman. He created them to be equal partners. God gave each gender different attributes, so they would complete one another in unity and harmony. God did give the role of headship to the husband, but because of the fall, man's sinful nature turned submission into a struggle for power and control over his mate.

Submission is *not*: domination, subjugation, a dictatorship, or bondage. Contrary to popular opinion, from God's perspective, submission is not a bad word. Instead, under the proper conditions, it's a beautiful expression of genuine love. Submission is not a putdown for women; it's simply the way spiritual reality works—a governing principle instituted by God for the harmony of His kingdom.[2] Submission works in God's plan, if we do it God's way. Abusive men turn the blessing of submission into a curse.

The Christian woman is in a state of confusion. She does not want to offend God by leaving her husband, so she stays and blames herself for his violent behavior. God hates the sin of domestic violence, but He loves the sinner. God does not allow sin to be covered up. Sin needs to be confessed. Real love does not excuse sin—real love confronts sin. (Once atomic-powered, my secret became weak when truth taught me how to speak.)[2] God's truth is THE truth. Just as God exposed the sin of King David, when he committed adultery with Bathsheba and murdered her husband, God will expose the sin of domestic violence. "Whatever is hidden will be revealed." (Luke 12:2) It is not an honor to be martyred by your husband. Dying or being abused at the hands of your spouse serves no purpose in the kingdom of Heaven.

Verbal abuse
- yelling
- uses profanity
- criticizes appearance
- name calling
- degrades women
- condescending laughter
- threatens to hurt her
- uses sarcasm
- threatens to hurt their children

She is criticized with words that cut deeply. He often criticizes her in front of their children, friends, and family members. "You are stupid, fat, and ugly." These comments about her physical appearance and weight are used to lower her self-concept. When he gets angry, he shouts profanities. His tone of voice is often condescending and mocking. Compliments are very rare or non-existent. Verbal abuse also includes threats of physical abuse and/or threats about taking the children away if she ever leaves him. Proverbs 18:21 states that death and life are in the power of the tongue. Words *do* hurt; they wound her soul and spirit. James 3:8-10 states, "But no one can tame the tongue; it is a restless evil and full of deadly poison. With it we bless our Lord and Father; and with it we curse men, who have been made in the likeness of God; from the same mouth come both blessing and cursing. My brethren, these things ought not to be this way."

The batterer downgrades women in general, and often tells demeaning sexual jokes. He has a low opinion of the value of women in society. He may verbally or sexually harass his female co-workers. Psalms 55:21:

"The words of his mouth were smoother than cream or butter, but war was in his heart; his words were softer than oil, yet they were drawn swords." (NIV) Verbal abuse is tremendously toxic when combined with physical abuse.

Sexual abuse
- forcing unwanted sexual acts
- forcing wives to watch pornography
- making demeaning sexual remarks
- committing incest
- wanting sex after the abuse
- adultery
- assaulting breasts or genitals
- treating others as sexual objects
- forcing sadistic sexual acts
- forced pregnancy or abortion
- marital rape
- excessive flirting with other women
- constant sexual demands
- withholding sexual relations

Sex is expected on demand. If the wife refuses for any reason, she is often forced to submit, in an act of marital rape. Sometimes the husband is addicted to pornography and forces his wife to watch the movies with him. There is also the opposite behavior, when the husband denies his wife sexual relations and blames it on her weight and appearance.

Social abuse
- forbids her to invite friends to their home
- forbids her to speak to others when he is not around
- forbids her to talk on the phone to old friends

The social abuser isolates his wife from her family and friends. He monitors her trips to the grocery store, doctor visits, and church outings; or, using the excuse that the family only needs or can afford one car, forces her to stay home all day. He may forbid her to see the mail each day until after he has read it, or check on her at home by calling several times during the day. She is questioned at the end of each day about whom she talked to and what they said. She is falsely accused of flirting with other men when they go out to dinner or to the grocery store. He may force her to quit her job, or purposely jeopardize her employment by constantly calling and harassing her. He may falsely accuse her girlfriends of being lesbians to discredit and terminate her friendships.

- 74% of battered women are harassed at work either by phone or in person. (Westchester County Business Journal, Vol. 35, 08-05-1996, p. 13)

- 96% of employed battered women experience problems at work due to abuse from a partner. (National Victims Center, Employee Liability for Workplace Violence, 1996)

Economic abuse
- controlling money
- withholding child support
- hiding her car keys
- withholding financial information
- disabling car so she cannot go to work
- running up debts

The economic abuser has complete control over the checkbook and the finances. She is given money to buy groceries and household items only, and must ask him for money if she needs to purchase personal items. He often keeps his income a secret. He may refuse to let her find a part-time job outside the home because he would lose control of her daily activities.

Another type of economic abuse occurs when the husband is physically able to work but will not, and so does not financially support his family. The wife works, while he spends the day watching television, drinking alcohol, and playing cards with his unemployed friends. Economic abuse also happens to women who are not married but who are living with a man. She receives TANF (Temporary Aid for Needy Families), food stamps, and a medical card. Economic abuse is happening when the welfare check comes in the mail but by the tenth day of the month he is gone—he is kind and loving to her until the money runs out. The cycle continues. She sees the pattern, but allows him to manipulate her over and over again because she cannot stand to be lonely. Her self-esteem is at the bottom of the barrel. She hates herself for being weak and taking from her children to give to him. 2 Timothy 5:8 states, "A man who does not work is worse than an infidel."

Parental authority abuse
- undermines her authority with their children
- verbally and/or physically abuses her in front of the children
- allows the children to criticize her
- forbids her to discipline the children

He makes the decisions concerning the children and discipline, or he totally ignores them. Often the children are taught to spy on her behaviors and report back to him. She is the main caretaker, who feeds, bathes, and watches the children constantly, while he takes little or no responsibility for childcare. Eventually the male children may begin to abuse their mother physically, and the female children may verbally abuse her.

Are wives actually being murdered by their husbands?
YES! Read the following statistics:
- Homicide is the leading cause of on-the-job death for women. Some twenty percent of women killed on the job were murdered by their husband or former male partner. (Westchester County Business Journal, Vol. 35, 08-05-1996, p. 13)
- The FBI estimates that a woman is beaten in the United States every 15 to 18 seconds.
- Estimates indicate that 2,000 to 4,000 women are killed annually by husbands or partners.
- Women who leave their batterers are at seventy-five percent greater risk of being killed by the batterer than those who stay. (National Coalition Against Domestic Violence, Denver, CO.)
- Between fifteen and twenty-five percent of battered women were beaten while pregnant. (National Coalition Against Domestic Violence, Denver, CO.)
- In 1984 the United States Surgeon General declared domestic violence to be this nation's number one health problem.
- Four thousand women die each year from domestic violence.

Many women are threatened with guns, knives, and axes. For them, there is a real threat of death because of the seriousness of the abuse. Some batterers deliberately kill their wives, while some kill them accidentally through serious physical abuse.

What about the children and teens in violent homes?
Statistics from the National Coalition Against Domestic Violence show that:
- 73% of male abusers were abused as children.
- 80% of the men in prison grew up in a violent home.
- Of the children who witness domestic violence, 60% of the boys will eventually become batterers and 50% of the girls will become victims.
- Sixty-three percent of boys aged eleven to twenty years who commit homicide, murder the man who was abusing their mother.
- In at least one-half of wife-abusing families, the children are battered as well.

"...Anyone who lives in a violent home experiences an essential loss. The one place on earth where they should feel safe and secure has become a place of danger. The shadow of domestic violence has fallen across their lives, and they are forever changed." (U.S. Attorney General's Task Force Report on Family Violence, September 1984)

True Story

Jane attended church regularly until her first marriage. Her mother and father were active church members. Jane's visits to church were sporadic. Her second marriage was to weekend alcoholic who was not a Christian. Jane's two sons adored Ben. He did not abuse the children. One night, Jane and Ben's usual arguing and screaming match turned into a tragedy. Ben stumbled home, late again from a night of drinking alcohol with his buddies. The shoving and pushing turned into violence. Jane's teenage son full of fear, grabbed the hunting rifle and shot his stepfather. Ben survived, but would the marriage and the family?

Chapter Two

Crisis Intervention

Safety first is the first rule

Helpers (clergy, counselors, and laity) need to be aware of the seriousness of crisis intervention involving domestic violence, and they need to be well trained. Just because you have known the man for years does not mean he will not turn against you if you try to help his wife and family. He may interpret your intervention as betrayal. All helpers need to be educated on the state and federal laws concerning domestic violence, police intervention, and the court system. Helpers also need to be aware of community resources and social service agencies. Connecting victims and batterers with specialized agencies is a major part of crisis intervention.

Please seek counsel from a domestic violence shelter or coalition before you advise victims to temporarily or permanently leave the batterer. This can be the most crucial time for them, as studies show that the batterer is more likely to kill her because she is leaving him. He goes into a violent rage because he does not want to lose the control he has over her. He may hurt or kill anyone who gets in the way of his goal to bring her back or to kill her. This is the ultimate control—control over her life or her death. The murder may or may not be premeditated.

What causes a wife to ask for help at any given point, when she has been living with the abuse for a certain number of months or years? The abuse usually continues to escalate, causing the beatings to become more severe. He may start physically abusing the children, while in the past he used verbal and emotional abuse only. She may believe he is going to kill her, and she wants to leave. There may be a precipitating event that triggers her emotional intensity.

She may realize she is suicidal and wants help before she kills herself. She may realize she is homicidal and wants help before she kills her husband/boyfriend. He may bring a weapon into the home for the first time to try to control her by fear. Perhaps her denial of the problem is over and she is facing the reality of the abuse for the first time.

She may have called a hotline and received encouragement and support, and now believe there is hope for her problem. There are many reasons why a woman makes the decision to leave and seek help at a particular time in her life.

Where do the husbands stay during the process of counseling, until restoration is complete and permanent safety is established? Usually the wives and children seek safety at a domestic violence shelter and the husband stays in the home. He refuses to leave because he wants his family back. The family is forced to seek public housing if he does not stop the abuse.

A few men stay with parents, relatives or friends. Men who are financially stable may temporarily rent a small apartment or room. These men will do anything to get their families back. Allowing the wife and children to stay in the home without harassing them is a positive sign that the batterer wants to accept help.

There is an urgent need for transitional houses for the recovering batterers who cannot financially afford to support two homes during the period of separation. Churches and Christian organizations need to unite and help fund Christian transitional houses in each county. Husbands would keep their jobs and support their families while attending Christian counseling and a support/treatment/education group for male batterers. The wives and children would remain in the home. Maintaining a stable environment is better for the children: same school, friends, church, and neighborhood. The male batterer should suffer the consequences of temporarily leaving the home environment, not his children or wife.

How Did Jesus Handle a Crisis?

He dealt with people in different ways and related to people at different levels.

- He met their particular need at the time they needed it.
- He used different methods to heal people.
- He was compassionate and he gave hope.
- He was gentle or he was firm.
- He used confrontation when necessary.
- He asked questions, wanting people to think about the situation and to look for deeper truths.
- He was encouraging.
- He focused on their spiritual condition and dealt with their thoughts and behaviors.
- He endorsed the right behavior at all times.
- He used mercy but also justice.

- He went to the heart of the problem–he looked at the sin and the solutions for sin.
- He provided for their physical needs.
- He focused on the whole person.

We also need to address the physical, emotional, and spiritual needs of the victims of domestic violence. When the religious leaders brought the woman caught in the act of adultery to him, what did Jesus do? He dispelled the rioting crowd with the words of truth. "You who have never sinned, you cast the first stone." He was calm. He did not need to shout. He did not preach to the crowd. He did not verbally discipline the woman in front of the crowd. He did not pull out his counseling manual and turn to the chapter about conflict resolution. He gave the religious leaders a chance to rethink the consequences for her sin by making them examine their own sin. Slowly they slipped away as Jesus kneeled and wrote in the sand. What did He write in the sand? He may have written, "Where is the man who was committing adultery with the woman?" he then told the woman to go and sin no more. He told her to change her lifestyle. He gave her biblical principles and truth.

The Bible is full of people who dealt with crisis. From Genesis to Revelation and from Adam to the apostles, the Bible is a crisis intervention manual.

There are no emergencies to God because He is omniscient and know what is going to happen. However, God does not interfere with a person's will to make choices, good or bad.

A crisis is an opportunity for change for the victim and the batterer. A crisis turns on the heat; especially if police intervention is necessary. A batterer faces the reality that he could lose his family and his freedom. Jesus can use a crisis to bring about change. Our English word *crisis* comes from the Greek word *krisis*, which means "a decision point."

Scenarios

- You are the pastor of a large church. One night the wife of one of your deacons knocks on your door. She has a bloody face. Her two small children are with her. She is sobbing uncontrollably and says she is afraid her husband may try to kill her.

- Tim, a member of your Sunday school class, comes to you in embarrassment. He says his wife Jill explodes every three months and hits him. Jill also breaks his possessions and threatens to divorce him. Jill and Tim have attended their Sunday school class together for six months.

- Bob, a member of your congregation, has a reputation for his quick temper. His wife, Carol, plays the organ on Sundays at the church where you are the pastor. You have known both of them for three years. Lately, Carol has called in sick on Sundays. Some of the church ladies come to you because they have noticed bruises on Carol's face and arms. Carol says she fell or ran into the door.

- Sally and her three children have been attending your church for one year. You are the pastor of a small country church. You have never met her husband. Sally asked you not to visit her home, because Jim is not a Christian and doesn't like preachers. One day Sally confides in her Sunday school teacher that Jim is an alcoholic and gets drunk every two weeks with the paycheck. He is abusive to Sally when he is intoxicated. He pushes her and pulls her hair. The physical violence is becoming worse. Sally doesn't know what to do. She wants to be a good Christian wife. Sally has never worked outside the home. No one knows that Jim has been abusing her for five years.

- You are the assistant pastor at a church in the inner city. The pastor's wife has stopped attending church. She will not accept any telephone calls or talk to any church members. The senior pastor has been upset and distressed. He confides in you and says he accidentally broke her nose. He says he didn't mean to do it, and he's very sorry.

- Mike, one of the teenagers in the youth group, confided in the youth pastor that his stepfather beats on his mom. Mike says he has a knife and will kill his stepfather the next time he beats his mom.

- Mary comes to you for help. Her 22-year-old daughter is living with a man who physically and emotionally abuses her. Mary is afraid the boyfriend will seriously hurt her daughter.

- Dana, a 15-year-old teenager in the youth group, is dating Ken, an 18-year-old male. Ken is extremely jealous. When he goes into a jealous rage, he pushes and pinches Dana.

Assessment of the crisis situation

Questions to ask the victim about the situation:
- Does the spouse/boyfriend own any weapons (guns, knives, etc.)?
- Did he threaten you with a weapon?
- Was he drinking alcohol and/or taking drugs?
- How long has he been violent?
- What kind of violent acts did he do to you?
- Did he hurt the children by hitting or pushing them?
- Does he know where you are right now?
- Have you ever called the police before about the violence?
- Do you want to call the police right now?
- How can I help you?

What can you as a pastor or helper do to help the victim in crisis?

Options:
- Safety first is the first rule—safety for both victims and helpers.
    1. Call a domestic violence shelter to see if they have vacancies. Helpers recommend this option first. If there is no room available at the shelter in your county, the staff can try to find room at another shelter in a neighboring county.
    2. Many YWCA organizations have shelter programs for battered women.
    3. Call a 24-hour mental health crisis center. They usually have a respite room where the wife and children can stay for 24 hours.
    4. Discuss any situation involving teenagers and violence with the parents immediately. Report death threats to the proper authorities.

If no rooms are available at the above agencies:
1. Call her relatives if their house would be a place of safety.
2. Pay for a motel for the night for the wife and children. Do not tell the location to the batterer.

3. Allow the wife and children to stay with you and your family for the night if there is safety for all parties.
4. Call another designated church member and ask if the wife and children can stay one night, but only if there is no chance of violence to the member from the abuser.

- Medical treatment is the second rule.
    1. Does the wife or children need medical treatment?
    2. Does the wife or children have any prior serious medical conditions?
    3. Do they need prescription medication?
    4. Take pictures of any injuries to use in court if necessary.
    5. Record the date, time, and facts about the incident.

Options:
1. Transport them to the local emergency room if necessary.
2. Transport them to an emergency room out of town if there is immediate danger from the abuser.
3. Call 911 for an ambulance.
4. Call her family physician if there is a medical history of serious illness and a need for urgent treatment.

Police intervention may be necessary.
   Options:
      1. Encourage the victim to call the police.
      2. You call the police and report the incident.

Prayer is needed.
      1. Pray for the safety of the women, children, helpers, police and batterers.
      2. Pray for the power of the Holy Spirit to intervene.

What can you as a pastor or helper do to help the batterer?
   Options:
   The actions you take during a crisis situation will be determined by the victim's answers to the assessment questions. If you know the batterer, and there is no danger to your physical safety:
   1. Go to the batterer's home. Take a few men from the church with you. Assess the situation. Is the man intoxicated, suicidal, or homicidal?

2. Assure him that his family is safe and you want to help.
3. Insist that his family spend the night away from him.
4. Offer a plan for intervention with several options: counseling, Christian male support/ treatment/ education group, and future marital counseling.

If you do not know the batterer or if there is a weapon and/or death threats:
1. Police intervention is absolutely necessary.
2. The best option for the family is a domestic violence shelter. If your county does not have a shelter, call the nearest shelter in another county and ask if they have room for the victims. Shelters will contact other shelters and try to find a place for the victims. The staff will ask you to transport the victim to the police station, or the police will transport the victims to the shelter. The locations of shelters are kept secret at all times for safety and protection.

Batterers are experts at manipulation. Do not allow them to manipulate you about the seriousness of the abusive situation. The batterer may be paranoid and actually believe his wife is being unfaithful. He will try to get you to take his side. He may cry, beg, and plead with you to tell him where his family is staying, but you must <u>not</u> tell him. He may threaten his own suicide if his spouse does not return. If he threatens suicide, transport him to a 24-hour mental health crisis center or a hospital emergency room. Do not leave him alone until the crisis is over.

How will a domestic violence shelter help the women and children?
1. The shelter will provide safety. The location is unknown to the community.
2. The shelter will provide food, clothing, and personal items.
3. The staff will provide emotional support and counseling.
4. The staff will educate her about domestic violence. It is the woman's decision to stay or leave the shelter at any time.
5. The staff will provide information about her legal rights. She can file domestic violence charges through the Municipal Court for criminal charges, or she can file through the Common Pleas Court. Legal Aid services are also available. The staff will make the appointment and transport her.

6. They will help her file a Civil Protection Order.
7. They will help her to sign up for welfare through the Dept. of Human Services. She can apply for food stamps and medical cards.
8. They will help her to locate public housing or an apartment if necessary.

Although most shelters are not Christian-based, the staff are trained professionals who provide intervention, prevention, and education to the victims and children. Many of the staff members are women of faith. A Christian-based domestic violence shelter will offer biblical counseling to the victims, and the batterers will be referred to a Christian male support/ treatment/education group. Psalms 31:20 states: "Thou dost hide them in the secret place of Thy presence from the conspiracies of man; Thou dost keep them secretly in a shelter from the strife of tongues."

Family counseling can begin ONLY after the violence stops and the batterer attends therapy. The safety of the wife and children must always be the first and major priority.

NOTE: In a majority of cases, when a victim enters a shelter, she wants her counselor to tell her whether or not she should get a divorce. The choice belongs to the client—it is her decision. Staff members should not coerce any client to seek a divorce.

What can the pastors/helpers do to help?
1. It is very important that the women continue to receive emotional support from the pastor or helper while they are in the shelter. They need to know their church family supports and believes them.
2. Use additional community resources for families in crisis. Give the victims information about legal, medical, and financial resources. Middle-income to upper-income families usually do not know about the free community resources that are available.
3. Help the abuser to find a temporary place to live while the process of healing and restoration takes place. It is easier for the children if the father leaves the home until safety is established and assured. He needs to continue to work to support his family financially.
4. Offer weekly counseling sessions or refer him to a Christian counselor. Domestic violence counseling is not marital counseling.
5. Refer him to a Christian male support/treatment/education group for batterers.

6. Follow up on his treatment.
7. Hold him accountable in your church. Ask him to resign from any Church positions until restoration is completed.

Confidentiality issues:

If a victim confides in you about her husband's abusive behaviors and asks you not to confront him, then please do as she asks. You could put her in danger by revealing her story to the abuser. She needs to have a safety plan in place before he is confronted. Do not attempt to offer marital counseling at this time. If the victim reveals the abuse in a session, she may be beaten after the couple leaves your office. The batterer will deny the abuse.

What if she returns to the batterer?

The wife/girlfriend may go back to the abuser. The past has taught helpers that most victims leave and return to the abuser an average of seven times before they permanently leave the situation. This fact is very frustrating for helpers, as well as for family and friends. We cannot force her to seek help, but we can be there with support when she finally does seek intervention. We cannot force treatment upon the victims or batterers. We can ask for police intervention, but the judge and the court system must order, enforce, and monitor counseling for the abuser. Helpers are mandated by law to report suspected child abuse. It is our duty to help the children.

Crisis phone calls from victims

One of your church members calls you on the telephone and says she needs help, that her husband is being abusive. What do you do?

First, assess the situation with brief questions:
- Are you or your children in danger right now?
- Is your husband there now?
- Does he have a weapon? Is he intoxicated?
- Do you or the children need medical attention?
- Do you want me to call the police? Can you call the police?
- Does your husband know you called me?
- Can you safely leave the house?
- Do you want me to call anyone for you?

Options:
1. Call the police, identify yourself, and ask them to meet you there.
2. Ask the wife to call the police if possible. The police can transport her to the police station, where she will be transported to a shelter by a shelter staff worker.
3. Go to the house and find a temporary place for the husband to stay, but only if it is safe and the wife and children are out.
4. Suggest the wife leave the house with the children and go to a safe place.

Educate yourself on the signs of spousal abuse for quick intervention:
- Frequent visits to the emergency room
- A history of miscarriages
- Bruises. She makes excuses, such as she fell or ran into a door.
- Anxiety
- Isolated from friends, church, and family members
- Does not talk to other men at church
- No direct eye contact
- Often appears sad and depressed
- Frequent headaches or other physical illnesses
- Takes total responsibility for caring for the children

Look for patterns of behavior, not isolated incidents.

What do you do when the husband is holding his wife and children hostage in their own home?

Options:
1. Call police immediately and report the situation. "I'm Pastor Jones of the United Church of Jesus, and I want to report a church member is being held hostage in her home by her husband." Give the police information about the family, including their address. Call a domestic violence shelter for intervention immediately.
2. Safety for the pastor and helpers is of utmost importance in a hostage situation. Only go to the home if the police are there. Assist the wife and children only after the police take the abuser to jail.
3. Call Children's Protective Services if children are being held hostage.

Behaviors that precede a hostage situation:
- The husband follows her into the bathroom while she showers, etc.
- He takes the telephone to work with him.
- He tears up her good clothes.
- He takes her car keys.
- He takes all the money, the checkbook, and the credit cards.
- She cannot go to the grocery store without him.
- She is told not to call or visit any of her family members.
- He asks the children to spy on her and report back to him.
- He tells her not to get the mail out of the mailbox.
- He tells her not to go outside while he is at work. The curtains are to stay shut.
- He misses work to stay home and monitor her activities.
- He calls her several times a day and expects her to answer the phone by the second ring.
- He quits his job to stay home and watch her.
- He takes her name off the checking and savings accounts.
- He comes home for lunch every day to check up on her.
- He keeps the children home from school.
- He moves the family around to different areas and isolates them from friends and family.
- His accusations and false beliefs about his wife committing adultery are intensified.
- He leaves an unloaded gun on the kitchen table while he is at work, to threaten her.
- He leaves a bullet from his gun in the bedroom as a symbol of control.
- He kills the family pet and implies that this will happen to her if she ever leaves him.

A hostage situation evolves over a period of time, and the batterer should be considered dangerous. Helpers and victims need to be aware of the precipitating behaviors of the batterer to prevent a hostage situation. His purpose is to exercise total control over his wife and/or children.

Safety plan and emergency kit for victims of domestic violence

For women and children who need to temporarily leave their homes due to fear of physical violence and safety issues, a safety plan is im-

perative. Keep the following items at a friend's house or hidden at your house:
- Extra keys for house and car
- Cash
- A bag with extra clothing for you and children
- Any prescription medicine for you or children
- Important phone numbers

Only keep these items at your house as a last option. The abuser may search and find them.

Important documents and information:
- Bank and checking account information
- Credit card information
- Social Security numbers of children and spouse
- Spouse's date of birth
- Birth certificates
- Marriage license
- Driver's license
- Health insurance card and policy information
- Children's school records and medical records: immunization cards
- Passports, Green card, work permits
- Address book
- Children's favorite toys

Tell your pastor, family and friends that you are temporarily leaving. Do not tell your friends and family where you are going. The abuser may threaten and harass them. They can honestly say they do not know where you are staying.

Be sure to park in a place where your spouse cannot recognize your car. Shelters have hidden places for victims to park their cars. You may go to a police station and an officer can transport you and the children to a domestic violence shelter, or a shelter staff member will pick you up at the police station and transport you to the shelter.

Do not leave behind the phone numbers to any domestic violence shelters. The abuser may try to locate you. Do not plan on writing checks or using a credit card, because he may be able to trace your location through them. Victims in a confidential location may unknowingly reveal their location to the abuser—Caller ID and Automatic Callback put the staff and volunteers of domestic violence hotlines, shelters, and programs at risk. The situation could also be dangerous for family, friends, pastors, counselors, and helpers. The telephone is generally the tool that victims use to seek help. Keep a cellular phone with you at all times.

Call the children's school and briefly explain that they will be out of school for awhile. The children will be able to attend school in the county and district where the shelter is located. Seek counsel from the shelter staff if the husband has threatened to kidnap the children. Court proceedings for custody can start immediately.

Safety issues for victims

If the batterer does not accept intervention and counseling and continues to stalk you after you leave the shelter:
- See section about laws on domestic violence and stalking for legal intervention. Call your state domestic violence coalition for information about the laws in your state. Laws vary from state to state. Use police, the courts, and the criminal justice system.
- Install a home security system.
- Change locks on all doors and install deadbolt locks on all doors.
- Install locks on all windows.
- Install outside safety lights.
- Install an alarm system in your home and car.
- Change residence and move to a safer location.
- Teach your children an escape plan, in case the abuser breaks into your home. Teach them to dial 911 or to alert a designated neighbor. Install a telephone in their rooms.
- Carry a cellular phone at all times.
- Alert your neighbors to the color and model of his car. Instruct them to call police if he trespasses on your property. Show them his picture for identification.
- Buy a watchdog.
- Keep your car locked at all times.
- Take self-defense classes.
- Alert your employer and co-workers about his stalking behaviors. Show his picture to them, and tell them to call the police if he trespasses.
- Do not go out alone at night until he stops stalking you.
- Under certain circumstances, it may be necessary to disappear completely and change your name and social security number. There is help available, if this is an option.
- Keep a written record of his stalking activities.

- Keep a copy of your protection order with you at all times. Make extra copies and keep them in a safe place.
- Call the police if your abuser violates the protection order.
- If your protection order is out of state, register it with local police and/or clerk of courts.
- Give copies of your protection order to anyone with whom your children may stay (schools, babysitter, etc.).
- Use the blocking code when making telephone calls by dialing #67 or its equivalent. This prevents batterers from using "Caller ID" to monitor your calls.
- Obtain an unlisted phone number.
- Rent a post office box for mail.
- Take safety classes if you purchase a gun.
- Assess the potential lethality of the batterer. There is an increased risk of assault and murder if the batterer abuses alcohol or drugs, possesses weapons, stalks you, or verbally threatens suicide or homicide.

Child abuse assessment*

Who are the mandated reporters?

Certain professionals are mandated to report when acting in their official or professional capacities, if they suspect a child may be abused or neglected. If they fail to report, they could be found guilty of a fourth-degree misdemeanor and liable for civil damages.

clergy	audiologists
child care workers	coroners
social workers	podiatrists
school authorities	school employees
day care personnel	school teachers
dentists	psychologists
nurses/other health care personnel	speech pathologists
children's services personnel	counselors
attorneys	physicians, interns, residents
officers and employees of any county	

Some states do not legally require ministers to report suspected child abuse, but I believe it is our ethical duty as ministers to immediately report the disclosure of child abuse to the appropriate state agencies. Check with your county child protection agency on the laws in your state.

How do I report suspected abuse or neglect?
You should report any child under 18 years of age, or any physically or mentally handicapped child under age 21, whom you have reason to believe has suffered any wound, injury, disability, or condition of such nature as to indicate abuse or neglect. You are not required to show physical proof or other forms of proof. It is the responsibility of the investigatory agency to determine if abuse or neglect is occurring.

Before you report suspected child abuse, inform your client and/or church member that you are under obligation to immediately make a report to the appropriate state agency. Explain the procedure and give information to help him/her better understand the process of the investigation. Continue to offer emotional and spiritual support to all family members.

Where do I report suspected abuse or neglect?
A report may be made by telephone, in person, or in writing to the County Children's Services. This phone number will be listed in the local phone book, or call your local information directory.

Information to report:
- The name and address of the child you suspect is being abused or neglected. The age of the child and birth date, if available.
- The name and address of the parent or caretaker.
- The name and address of the person you suspect is abusing or neglecting the child.
- The reason you suspect the child is being abused or neglected.
- Any other information which may be helpful to the investigation.

You may report anonymously. Giving your name provides documentation that you, as a mandated reporter, followed the law.

How is child abuse or neglect defined?
- Physical abuse: the non-accidental injury of a child.
- Sexual abuse: any act of a sexual nature upon or with a child.
- Emotional abuse: chronic attitude or acts which interfere with the psychological and social development of the child.

- Physical neglect: failure to meet the requirements basic to a child's physical development, such as supervision, housing, clothing, medical attention, nutrition, and support.
- Emotional neglect: failure to provide the support or affection necessary to a child's psychological and social development.

This section is not meant to be an exhaustive resource for information about child abuse and neglect. Please see the appendix for a list of resources for further information.

*Information taken from the *Ohio Children's Trust Fund: A Guide for Mandated Reporters, Child Abuse and Neglect*. Laws vary from state to state. Check the laws in your state about who is a mandated reporter.

To The Victims:

If your husband is physically abusing the children and you have witnessed the abuse, you are at risk to temporarily and/or permanently have the children removed from your home if the abuse is reported to Children's Services and their investigation is validated by proof.

Christian women often function as the referee between the batterer and the children. They often battle their husbands to intercept the blows meant for the children. The reason Christian women stay, even though their children are being abused, is very different from the reasons non-Christian women stay—women in religious homes are trying to obey their husbands. To the mandated agencies, however, this reason is not valid. The court system will not consider your Christian values as a valid reason to stay in a home when your children are being physically abused.

Christian women, you must seek safety if your husband/partner is physically abusing the children. If you don't, the children may be seriously injured, and you are at risk to lose your children to foster care. Please leave and seek help the very first time your husband/partner physically abuses the children.

Why do women stay?

The basic reason is fear. He often threatens to kill her if she ever leaves. He may threaten to kill her parents or to kidnap the children and says she will never see them again. She doesn't know if he will or won't. She keeps hoping her husband will change. He plays "mind games," and she may believe she causes his violent behavior.

She eventually believes his lies: She's worthless. She's lazy. She's a terrible mother. She is brainwashed by him. She sinks deeper and deeper into depression. The more control she gives him, the more her identity is lost.

Christian women believe in the sanctity and permanence of marriage. They are afraid of what the church will think. They do not want to be excommunicated from their church family. They are embarrassed. They do not want to be divorced. They love their husbands, but they hate the violence. They know he needs counseling, and they feel sorry for him.

Some parents and relatives in regional areas are not supportive of women leaving the abuser. Some women are products of generational domestic violence. Violence is a "normal" part of life for them. The family may tell her to stay and try to be a better wife. Some counties do not have domestic violence shelters. Country towns do not have public transportation.

Many women stay because they have little money or resources. The husband controls all the finances. Some women have little or no job training or college education. The thought of working terrifies them when they have never worked outside the home.

Some women have a low reading level, a learning disability, or a physical handicap. A few cannot read. These factors are sometimes overlooked by helpers. Immigrants are falsely threatened with deportation by their spouses if they leave. Some husbands purposely never obtain legal status for their mates, so they can exercise a real threat of deportation.

Many of the women do not know their behavior can be labeled as codependency—negative thinking which keeps them in destructive relationships. (See section on codependency.)

She may have a fear that people will not believe her. He may be an outstanding community leader, a police officer, or pastor of a large church. She has never told even one person about her deadly secret.

Considering the effects of the new welfare reforms at the federal and state levels, it is imperative that church communities become involved in helping abused women. They may not seek help without the safety net of welfare, food stamps, and medical cards. As a social worker, I do believe in changing the external environment, either temporarily or permanently, for the betterment of the family. As a minister, I also know that internal change MUST be through the life-changing power of Jesus Christ. The Christian community has long known that societal problems will not be cured by the hiring of more social workers. I believe the Christian community must help with the tangible physical needs of these women, men, and children. But equally important is the giving of spiritual knowledge.

The victims also fear homelessness for their children. Up to fifty percent of all homeless women and children in this country are fleeing domestic violence. (Elizabeth Schneider, *Legal Reform Efforts for Battered Women*, 1990).

The court system may have failed to protect her and her children the first time she tried to leave and press charges. It is common for the abuser to violate the protection orders. He may only batter her every three to four months. The rest of the time he tries not to be abusive. After each episode, he cries and begs forgiveness. She feels confused and wants to believe he will stop the violent behaviors.

Christian women stay because they are loving and nurturing wives. They believe they can change their husbands with unconditional love and prayer. Giving up on him is perceived as a personal failure.

She may believe that stress and financial problems are the cause of his violence, that when he makes a better income, he will stop the abuse. She believes this lie. She stays because of guilt, responsibility, and shame. The abuser treats everyone better than he does his own wife. A few women stay because they will not give up their houses, furniture, and possessions. Safety is the issue.

Women also stay because there are not enough domestic violence shelters in the United States. Where are these abused women and children supposed to go?

- Due to space limitations, for every one woman accepted into a battered women's shelter, two women and their children are turned away. In some urban areas, five to seven women are turned away for every two women served. (National Coalition Against Domestic Violence)
- There are nearly three times as many animal shelters in the United States as there are shelters for battered women. (Senate Judiciary Committee Hearings, 1990)

Funding is needed for the development of more shelters for crisis intervention. Church involvement is desperately needed for Christian shelters and transitional houses.

Clearly, there are many factors involved in why a woman stays in an abusive relationship. The Christian community needs to try to understand her reasons and, equally important, to try to understand why men batter.

SUICIDE ASSESSMENT

☐ yes 1. Do you think about killing yourself?
☐ no

☐ yes 2. Are your suicidal thoughts becoming more frequent?
☐ no

☐ yes 3. Do you have a plan to kill yourself?
☐ no

☐ yes 4. Do you have a definite time and location for killing yourself?
☐ no

☐ yes 5. Do you have access to medication/pills?
☐ no

☐ yes 6. Are you taking prescription medication for anxiety? (Valium,
☐ no   Librium, etc.)

☐ yes 7. Are you using alcohol or drugs?
☐ no

☐ yes 8. Do you have easy access to a gun or weapon?
☐ no

☐ yes 9. Are you asking God to take your life?
☐ no

☐ yes 10. Have you tried to kill yourself before?
☐ no

☐ yes 11. Do you feel helpless and hopeless?
☐ no

☐ yes 12. Have you stopped praying?
☐ no

☐ yes 13. Do you feel as if God is far away and doesn't care?
☐ no

☐ yes 14. Is it difficult to read your Bible?
☐ no

☐ yes 15. Are you isolating yourself from friends, relatives, and church?
☐ no

☐ yes 16. Is the abuse kept secret?
☐ no

☐ yes 17. Do you believe your children would be better off without
☐ no   you?

☐ yes 18. Do you believe the abuse from your husband/partner is
☐ no   your fault?

☐ yes 19. Is it difficult to get out of bed in the mornings?
☐ no

☐ yes 20. Are you going to kill yourself?
☐ no
☐ unsure

If you answered [yes] to any of the above questions, you must seek help immediately. Suicide is not the solution. Most victims who are suicidal do not want to die, they just want the pain to go away and the battering to stop. Being assaulted by your husband is not your fault. Your children would not be better off without you—they need their mother. You deserve to live without violence in your home. There is help available to you.

SEEK HELP NOW
1. Call a family member, friend, pastor, pastor's wife, counselor, or physician.
2. Call a domestic violence shelter locally or nationally.
3. Call a crisis hotline in your city, county, state, or nation.
4. Call 911.
5. Go to a domestic violence shelter or coalition.

6. Go to a hospital emergency room.
7. Go to a 24-hour crisis mental health center.
8. Drive or walk to your church and ask your pastor or church friend to pray with you and for you.
9. Remove the guns or weapons from your home or ask someone else to remove them.
10. Remove pills and medication from your home or ask someone else to remove them.
11. Repeat this scripture verse: "I can do all things through Christ Who strengthens me." (Philippians 4:13) There is power in the word of God.

Telephone number to the domestic violence shelter in my community is _____.

Telephone number to the crisis hotline in my state is _____.

Telephone number to a national crisis hotline is _____.

People I can call who will help me:

Name _____   Phone _____

Name _____   Phone _____

HOMICIDE ASSESSMENT

❏ yes 1. Do you have thoughts about killing your husband/partner?
❏ no

❏ yes 2. Are the thoughts about killing your husband/partner
❏ no   becoming more frequent?

❏ yes 3. Do you have easy access to a gun or weapon?
❏ no

❏ yes 4. Do you have a definite plan, time, and location for killing
❏ no   your husband/partner?

☐ yes 5. Are you using alcohol or drugs?
☐ no

☐ yes 6. If you are using alcohol or drugs, is the amount increasing?
☐ no

☐ yes 7. Are you addicted to prescription medication? (Valium,
☐ no   Librium, etc.)

☐ yes 8. Is the physical abuse from your husband/partner becoming
☐ no   more frequent and violent?

☐ yes 9. Is your husband/partner using alcohol or drugs?
☐ no

☐ yes 10. Is your husband/partner threatening to kill you?
☐ no

If you answered [yes] to any of the above questions, you must seek help immediately. Homicide is not the solution. There is help available for you. Many battered women are in prison for killing their husbands.

SEEK HELP NOW
1. Call a family member, friend, pastor, pastor's wife, counselor, or physician.
2. Call a domestic violence shelter locally or nationally.
3. Call a crisis hotline in your city, county, state, or nation.
4. Call 911.
5. Go to a 24-hour crisis mental health center.
6. Drive, take a bus or walk to your church and ask your pastor or church friend to pray with you and for you.
7. Only walk if it is safe and not late at night.
8. Remove the gun or weapons from your home or ask someone else to remove them.
9. Repeat this scripture verse: "I can do all things through Christ who strengthens me."

Domestic violence and federal laws

Battering men must be made to accept the sole responsibility for their physical violence. You batter—you go to jail. It is time for the Christian community to seek out intervention by police, judges, and the court systems. Treatment by the courts must be mandatory and enforced. Consequences must be applied for noncompliance by the batterers. We need the government and state to intervene due to the magnitude of domestic violence. The state can offer penalties and punishment, which are necessary tools; but the state cannot cure the violent internal anger and control issues of batterers. Only God can cure the inner anger and pathological power struggles of Christian men who abuse their wives and children.

Domestic violence affects society as a whole. God can use the secular society as another tool to fulfill His purpose to heal His families. God can use the police and court systems to aid pastors and helpers. 1 Peter 2:13 states, "Be submissive to every human institution and authority for the sake of the Lord..." (TAB) Police are not the enemies of the Christian community. It is not a weakness for the Christian community to ask for police intervention. Domestic violence laws are necessary to save lives. It is not a disgrace for Christian wives to ask for police protection. It takes courage and strength for the victims and pastors to reveal this ugly "wart" to secular society. We know we will be criticized and ridiculed by outsiders; but the fact remains that Christian men and pastors who physically assault their wives and children are not above the laws. Proverbs 19:19 states, "A man of great anger shall bear the penalty, for if you rescue him, you will only have to do it again."

Separation Violence

For a battered wife, leaving her husband increases the potential for violent assaults and even death. Up to seventy-five percent of domestic violence assaults reported to law enforcement agencies may be inflicted after separation of the couple. (U.S. Dept. of Justice, 1983) When a victim seeks intervention, a batterer perceives her action as betrayal and strikes back in retaliation. Violence escalates as he tries to coerce her into reconciliation.

The laws relating to domestic violence have drastically changed in the last fifteen years and continue to change. In 1982, Maryland was the first state to pass laws that made wife-beating a crime, punishable by 40 lashes or a year in jail.[1] Although technically no jurisdiction in this country now permits a husband to strike his wife or a man to assault his partner (U.S. Commission of Civil Rights, 1982), the reality is that men still use violence against wives without fear of police intervention or consequences.

Recent Developments in the Law

Civil protection orders in most jurisdictions are now broader and include the victim who is divorced, who is a current or former family or household member of the perpetrator, who is related by blood or marriage to the batterer, who is the parent of a child of the abuser, and who has been sexually or otherwise intimate with the abuser.[2] Civil protection orders can be effective only if they are properly issued and enforced by the police and the courts.

State statues now enable police to arrest without a warrant. With a warrantless arrest, it is possible to take a suspect into custody at the scene rather than trying to locate him after obtaining a warrant from the court. The perpetrator may be introduced into the criminal justice system earlier. Victims are better protected by prompt arrest, arraignment, and imposition of special bail conditions or criminal protective orders.[3]

Most domestic violence crimes involving injury should be classified as felonies, since injuries produced by domestic violence are as serious as those inflicted in ninety percent of all violent felonies (Attorney General's Family Violence Task Force of Pennsylvania, 1989). However, police still identify most domestic violence assaults as misdemeanors.

A majority of states have adopted statues requiring courts to consider domestic violence as a factor in custody and visitation determinations. Advocates for battered women have begun to engage in safety planning with the women and children to identify special needs when the abuser is allowed custodial access.[4]

In 1988, Congress amended the Victims of Crime Act, requiring state victim compensation programs to make awards to victims of domestic violence. The Violence Against Women Act (VAWA), passed as part of the Crime Act of 1994, is a landmark bipartisan legislation, combining tough new penalties with programs to prosecute offenders and help women victims of violence.[5] Key provisions of the VAWA:

- States must enforce protection orders issued by other states.
- There are federal penalties for an abuser who crosses state lines to violate a protection order and injure his/her partner.
- Federal sentences for repeat offenders may be increased to twice the authorized time.
- Provides $800 million in grants to state and local governments to improve law enforcement, prosecution, and victim services in cases of violent crimes against women. This includes domestic violence and sexual assault.

There are opposing viewpoints about domestic violence reforms. During the past few decades, criminal justice agencies have radically changed the ways they respond to domestic violence incidents. Arresting the batterer has become the preferred police response. Restraining orders have become more widely used. Court-mandated treatment for batterers has become common. Prosecutors have acted to charge the offender even if the victim backs out. Even with all the new changes, though, many professionals conclude that the criminal justice system remains inadequate in reducing domestic violence crimes.[6]

Check with your state and/or county domestic violence coalition/shelter for information about new laws concerning domestic violence in your state.

CRIMES OF DOMESTIC VIOLENCE
- DOMESTIC VIOLENCE
- MENACING BY STALKING
- AGGRAVATED TRESPASS
- VIOLATING A PROTECTION ORDER
- FELONIOUS ASSAULT
- AGGRAVATED ASSAULT

What is domestic violence?
Domestic violence includes the crimes of domestic violence, menacing by stalking, aggravated trespass, and violation of protection order. Domestic violence is one or more of the acts listed above and described below occurring between family or household members who have lived or are living together.

What acts are considered domestic violence in criminal or common pleas court?
1. Knowingly causing or attempting to cause physical harm to a family or household member

or
2. Recklessly causing serious physical harm to a family or household member
or
3. By threat of force, knowingly causing a family or household member to believe that the offender will cause imminent physical harm to the family or household member.

What acts are considered domestic violence in civil (domestic relations) court?
1. Attempting to cause or recklessly causing bodily injury to family or household member
or
2. Placing another person by threat of force in fear of imminent serious physical harm
or
3. Committing any act with respect to a child that would result in the child being considered an abused child. This would include:
   a) Sexual conduct or sexual contact
   b) Endangering the child by creating a substantial risk to the health or safety of the child;
   or
   c) Showing that any injury or death was inflicted by other than accidental means.

Who are considered family and household members?
1. Spouses
2. Former spouses
3. Persons living together as spouses or otherwise cohabiting, or who have cohabited within one year prior to the date domestic violence occurred
4. Parent, children or other persons related by blood or marriage who are living or have lived with the offender
5. The natural parent of any child of whom the offender is the other natural parent

What acts are considered to be stalking?
Engaging in a pattern of behavior that knowingly causes another person to believe that the offender will cause either physical harm or mental distress to the other person.

What acts are considered aggravated trespass?

Entering or remaining on another's land or premises, intending to commit a misdemeanor and causing the other person to believe that the offender will cause physical harm to that person.

What does it mean to violate a protection order?

Violation occurs when a person recklessly violates any of the terms of either a Temporary Protection Order issued by a Criminal Court or a Civil Protection Order issued by a civil court.

What relief is available to victims of domestic violence?

Any adult household member can seek relief from domestic violence either on his or her own behalf or for the benefit of another family or household member. In Ohio, there are two legal remedies—civil and criminal. Relief may be sought by:

1. Filing for a Petition for a Civil Protection Order (CPO) with the Domestic Violence Relations Division of the Court of Common Pleas. You do not have to file criminal charges in order to file for a CPO.

and/or

2. Filing a Complaint charging the crime of Domestic Violence with the Municipal Court, or requesting the City Attorney's office or County Prosecutor's Office to file a complaint charging the crime of Domestic Violence on your behalf. A police officer may also bring his charge in your behalf. Relief includes a Temporary Protection Order (TPO).

What is the difference between civil and criminal courts?

1. Domestic relations court has the responsibility of terminating marriages, determining child custody, and providing for a fair division of marital property. The court also has the responsibility of providing protection to victims of domestic violence.
2. Criminal court (Municipal Court or Common Pleas) has the responsibility of punishing and/or confining the abuser, in addition to the responsibility to protect you.

The charge of Domestic Violence is a misdemeanor of the first degree. This means that if the accused is found guilty, the maximum sentence the court may impose is six months and a $1,000.00 fine.

A felony charge of Domestic Violence is appropriate if the abuser has been previously convicted of domestic violence or assault on a family or household member. This is a felony of the fifth degree and is punishable by a term of imprisonment up to two years and a $42,500.00 fine.

If a serious injury has been inflicted, or if you have been threatened with a deadly weapon, a charge of felonious assault may be brought against the abuser. This is an aggravated felony of the second degree—a very serious offense.

There are many specific crimes addressing sexual offenses. If you believe a sexual offense has been committed, consult with the police department or the prosecutor's office to determine the severity of the offense. In Ohio, marital rape is a crime. Therefore, if you are married and are compelled to engage in sexual conduct by force or threat of force, rape may be an appropriate charge. Rape is an aggravated felony of the first degree.. The punishment for rape is extremely severe.

If any criminal offense has been committed with a firearm, there is a prescribed additional three-year mandatory prison sentence.

How do I obtain a Temporary Protection Order (TPO)?

When a criminal charge is filed, you should request that a "Motion for Temporary Protection Order" be filed with the Complaint. The court must conduct a hearing within twenty-four hours after the filing of a request for a TPO.

After you file your motion (request) for a TPO, you need to appear before a Municipal Court judge, who may issue the TPO. This will usually take place the next morning in Municipal Court.

(Reprinted with permission from the *Action Ohio Manual*, Columbus, Ohio, 1997)

Check with your state coalition about domestic violence laws in your state.

Victim Advocates are available to accompany abused women throughout court proceedings. Domestic violence shelters receive funding to hire advocates.

True Story

Millie arrived at the domestic violence shelter with her two daughters. She had left her husband a few times before and stayed with family members, but this was her first time at a shelter. The children arrived without any personal items. Harold sold all their toys and valuables to buy beer. After eleven years of abuse, Millie was tired. Harold had spent the entire welfare check on beer. The bill money was gone. They lived in the country with only relatives for neighbors. Millie didn't read or write well. Harold would not allow her to get a driver's license. He would not even allow her to go to the grocery store. Millie was able to attend the little country church with her girls. Once in awhile, Harold would show up drunk at the Sunday service and demand that Millie come home and fix his dinner. The usual pattern was for the pastor to send Harold home.

The only time Harold was arrested for domestic violence, his mother bailed him out of jail and blamed Millie. Millie's mother didn't want to get involved. Every night Harold would whisper to Millie, *"I'll kill you if you ever leave."* The scars on her head from being hit with beer bottles convinced her that Harold might just be serious.

Chapter Three

Christian Men Who Batter

Are Battering Men Christians?
1. Some do not claim to be Christians. Their wives are Christians caught in a violent marriage.
2. Some claim to be Christians, but have not accepted Jesus Christ as their Savior. They claim automatic Christianity because they are Americans and believe in God. They may or may not attend church services.
3. Some can be compared with the religious, pious Pharisees. They do not have a personal relationship with Jesus Christ, the son of God. They have not experienced a true conversion. They usually hold an office in church: deacon, elder, board member, or Sunday school teacher.
4. Some are Christians and have accepted Jesus as their personal Savior, but are influenced by:
   - the flesh (Romans 7:14-25)
   - the world (James 4:1-4)
   - demonic activity and spirit of control (Hebrews 3:12-13, 1 Peter 5:8)
   - generational curses, self-inflicted curses, and unconfessed sins (Exodus 20:5-6, Deuteronomy 5:9-10)
   - faulty theology (2 Corinthians 11:3-4)
   - undiagnosed or untreated mental illness
   - undiagnosed or untreated head trauma
   - unresolved, suppressed, and/or repressed memories of past childhood abuse that reprogrammed them into bondage
   - stunted spiritual growth (1 Corinthians 3:1-3, Hebrews 5:11-12)
5. Many Christian batterers are saved spiritually but still hurting emotionally. They have accepted Jesus Christ as Lord and savior, but they still carry around past emotional baggage and unhealed wounds. The following is an example: If you were a bad cook before you were saved, then you will still be a bad cook after salvation. People become good cooks by trial and error, reading cookbooks, and observing a chef or teacher prepare food. The same is true for Christians. The Holy Spirit, pastor, and Christian friends

are the teachers, the Bible is our cookbook, and trial and error shows us God's amazing grace, mercy, and forgiveness.

A right relationship with God, the Father, Son, and Holy Spirit is imperative to the recovering batterer, just as it is imperative to all Christians who desire to be Christ-like. As pastors, counselors, and helpers, it our responsibility to:
- present the plan of salvation if he is not saved
- help him to rededicate his life to Christ
- confront him in truth and love about his relationship to Christ and his legalism
- mentor him for spiritual growth and hold him accountable
- accompany him or refer him to a deliverance ministry if necessary
- refer him to a Christian psychiatrist/counselor if necessary
- refer him to seek medical help if necessary
- encourage him to consistently attend a Christian support/treatment/education group for male batterers
- introduce him to the indwelling Holy Spirit

We will better know the batterer's relationship with God when we offer him counseling and restoration. If he will not accept help and continues to physically assault his wife, then we know by his fruits he is in need of spiritual healing or he has not accepted Christ as his Savior. Many men desperately want help to stop the abuse. Counseling will determine his condition.

Characteristics of Christian Batterers
Battering men display consistent abusive behaviors that are not isolated incidents. They may have a few or many of the behaviors listed below.
- explosive anger with a short fuse
- alcohol or drug addiction, kept hidden from everyone but the wife
- dictatorship in parenting
- legalistic about religious topics
- see things in black-and-white, all-or-nothing terms
- controls bank account and finances
- often has financial difficulties
- lacks coping skills for stress
- blames others for his problems: family, boss, and society
- mild to severe paranoia

- extreme personality, either a loner or a charmer
- pathological lying
- extramarital affairs
- addiction to pornography
- perfectionist who lives by a schedule, i.e. dinner is at the same time every night, or else
- mild to severe jealousy—accuses wife of adultery or flirting
- pessimistic about life—frequent complaining and criticizing
- does not trust others, including wife
- has frequent conflict with boss and co-workers
- history of being fired for not getting along with others
- mild to severe gambling and/or playing lottery
- poor communication skills
- prejudice against minorities and other religions
- if a minority, he is paranoid that Caucasians are out to get him
- does not do housework, as he considers it a woman's job
- his wife is primary caretaker of the children
- very serious, with little time for recreation and fun
- not reliable and avoids work, or is a workaholic
- religious background in a negative, "fire and brimstone," guilt-producing church which taught the justice of God but did not teach His mercy
- history of childhood physical, verbal, emotional, spiritual, or sexual abuse
- raised in single-parent home by his mother
- abandoned by biological father
- raised by a father who was a batterer
- demeans women in general and does not value them

Misogyny

What is misogyny? It means the hatred of women by men. Dr. Margaret Rinck, in her book, *Christian Men Who Hate Women*, states:

> Christian men who hate women (religious misogynists) are in some ways more dangerous and destructive in their behavior than their non-Christian counterparts. Secular misogynists do not have the powerful, additional arsenal of church doctrines, God-talk, and the sanctioning of male authority, which comes with the idea of Christian marriage.[1]

Unhealthy Christian men use radar to "zero in" on passive women with traditional family values. They usually do not date assertive or aggressive women. They search for women with the same passive, weak qualities as their mothers. The cycle of abuse is recreated in their own marriages.

This type of batterer often "sweeps" a woman off her feet in a brief whirlwind romance before marriage. He starts the abuse during the honeymoon. Many women believe the Christian label worn by some men automatically depicts a godly person. The women are shocked when his true personality is manifested and portrays abuse.

Types of men who batter

"Approximately one-third of the men counseled (for battering) at Emerge are professional men who are well respected in their jobs and their communities. These have included doctors, psychologists, lawyers, ministers, and business executives." (*For Shelter and Beyond*, Massachusetts Coalition of Battered Women Service Groups, Boston, MA, 1990)

According to studies, the top five professions for male abusers are:
1. Military Men
2. Doctors
3. Lawyers
4. Police Officers
5. Pastors

Abusive men who crave power and control are drawn into these professions to feed their appetites. The prestige feeds their egos. They are usually competitive at sports, and they like to win at any cost. Galatians 6:3 states, "For if anyone thinks he is something when he is nothing, he deceives himself."

Many abusive men have personality traits that could be considered as narcissistic. *The Diagnostic and Statistical Manual of Mental Disorders (DSM-IV)* describes the person with a Narcissistic Personality Disorder:

> A pervasive pattern of grandiosity (in fantasy or behavior), need for admiration, and lack of empathy, beginning by early adulthood and present in a variety of contexts, as indicated by five (or more) of the following:
> 1. has a grandiose sense of self-importance (e.g., exaggerates achievements and talents, expects to be

recognized as superior without commensurate achievements)
2. is preoccupied with fantasies of unlimited success, power, brilliance, beauty, or ideal love
3. believes that he or she is "special" and unique and can only be understood by, or should associate with, other special or high-status people (or institutions)
4. requires excessive admiration
5. has a sense of entitlement, i.e. unreasonable expectations of especially favorable treatment or automatic compliance with his or her expectations
6. is interpersonally exploitative, i.e. takes advantage of others to achieve his or her own ends
7. lacks empathy, i.e. is unwilling to recognize or identify with the feelings and needs of others
8. is often envious of others or believes that others are envious of him or hershows arrogant, haughty behaviors or attitudes

Personality Disorders are enduring patterns of behavior which have an onset in adolescence or early adulthood and lead to distress or impairment. Certain types of personality disorders can also describe some Christian batterers:
1. Schizoid—a pattern of detachment from social relationships and a restricted range of emotional expression.
2. Antisocial—a pattern of disregard for, and violation of, the rights of others.
3. Borderline—a pattern of instability in interpersonal relationships and self-image, and marked impulsiveness.
4. Avoidant—a pattern of social inhibition, feelings of inadequacy, and hypersensitivity to criticism.[2]

Severe Head Trauma

A study conducted by the University of Massachusetts Medical Center's domestic violence research and treatment center found that sixty-one percent of men involved in marital violence have signs of severe head trauma. The frontal lobe is injured, which is involved in controlling impulse control. Most studies deal with battering as a learned behavior. Eighty percent of the males in a Minnesota violence-control program grew up in homes where they saw or were victims of physical, sexual, or other abuse.[3]

Different types of Christian men who batter

Type A
High Violence
- generational domestic violence
- physical, emotional, sexual abuse in childhood by family members
- alcoholism and drug abuse in family tree
- antisocial personality
- low self-esteem, depression, emotionally volatile
- rigid sex role attitudes
- rebellious against authority figures, criminal record, and history of fighting
- violent behavior inside and outside of home
- becomes a Christian as an adult, but continues to carry around past emotional memories and behaviors; continues to be abusive

Type B
Low to Medium Violence
- raised in an overly strict religious home; no movies, skating, or fun allowed
- father is a pastor, deacon, elder, or holds a position in a church
- mother is dominated by father, with emotional/verbal abuse in family
- only violent in his own home
- no extreme physical abuse, but physical discipline as a child
- ritual church attendance and expects total submission of wife
- usually becomes a minister, deacon, or holds a position in the church; carries a lot of anger towards God

Type C
Medium to High Violence
- not raised in a Christian home, but became a Christian later in life
- raised by his mother, without a father figure
- a loner with poor social skills who represses emotions
- low self-esteem, intense dependency needs, pathological jealousy
- past addiction to pornography throughout childhood
- past and/or current alcohol or drug abuse

- past emotional, physical, or sexual abuse by mother's boyfriend or other male
- military history
- usually makes a career out of the military.

Type D
Low Violence to High Violence
- spoiled as a child, with inconsistent and very little discipline
- narcissistic personality, self-centered and rebellious as a teenager
- raised in a Christian home and had to be made to attend church
- explosive anger, but uses it more to control and manipulate
- a charmer who is very handsome and attention-seeking
- commits adultery and lives by double standard
- believes men are entitled to special treatment
- denies he needs counseling; looks for a passive mate as a wife

Christian batterers may also be a mixture of the above types, with low, medium, or high violence.

Pastors who batter their wives

I've counseled pastors' wives who suffered abuse—physical, verbal, emotional, spiritual, sexual, economic, and parental authority. These women seek help only after the abuse has reached a point of extreme severity. Pastors' wives will tolerate years of domestic violence before they seek outside help.

There are cases in the United States in which pastors have been convicted of killing their spouses. You may have difficulty comprehending the fact that some ministers do beat their wives and even commit murder. Every profession has its share of batterers; the pulpit and the mission field are no exception. The same crisis intervention plan in this resource guide is recommended for pastors and missionaries. They should not be treated differently. They must step down from their positions until counseling and family restoration are completed. The church needs to have a written policy and procedure for conducting investigations on religious leaders who are accused of domestic violence. Church boards, deacon, elders, and the congregation must be told if their pastor is assaulting his wife. They must take action immediately. Helping your pastor to hide his violent behavior only perpetuates his problem and keeps him stuck in sin. People in the ministry have human imperfections like all of us. I am not here to stand in judgment; God will judge them. I offer both the batterers and the victims help, hope, and healing through Jesus Christ.

Power in the ministry must have holiness at its heart, or the result will be an elevated ego, selfishness, and evil. How Satan delights in abuse in pastors' homes!

Mother Theresa had no monetary wealth, owned no land, held no political office, had no husband; yet when she spoke, Popes and Presidents listened. It is a paradox, but in becoming powerless before God, she became powerful before men and women. Her position of authority guaranteed the obedience of her followers, but she did not misuse her power or authority. The Apostle Paul stated, "For when I am weak, then I am strong...Power is perfected in weakness." (2 Corinthians 12:9-10) "But God has chosen the foolish things of this world to shame the wise, and God has chosen the weak things of this world to shame things which are strong." (1 Corinthians 1:27)

God uses our weaknesses to show others that we are real. The Bible is full of people with human weaknesses. We must admit and accept our weaknesses, or we will be never be spiritually empowered. "Although He died on the cross in weakness, Jesus now lives by the mighty power of God. We, too, are weak, but we live in Him and have God's power..." (2 Corinthians 13:4, NLT)

Christians must hold their pastors accountable if abuse exists in the pastor's marriage. Pastors and religious professionals are not above God's law or state and federal laws. Often our pastors do not know where to seek earthly help. Pastors, just like social workers, counselors, and professionals in the "helping field," often are drawn because of their own painful pasts. They carry hidden pain into the marriage and the pulpit. Many of these pastors are saved spiritually but still hurting emotionally.

True Story

Carla and Brock were a military family. They both were Christians and attended church. Brock possessed an aggressive, strong, and domineering personality but there was no abuse in the marriage, until...Brock turned into a Mr.Hyde and Dr. Jekel after he returned from the Desert Storm gulf war. The last and most serious violent episode permanently injured Carla. Brock tried to snap her leg into two pieces. After her release from the hospital, Carla moved back to her hometown. Brock was reassigned to active duty in other country. Carla came to counseling with severe depression and a permanent limp in her leg. She filed for divorce.

Chapter Four

Women, Men, and The Bible

Roles of men and women

It is imperative to dispel the myths concerning the roles of Christian women and men. Future generations will benefit from learning a correct Biblical perspective. Men are capable of being nurturing and sensitive while still keeping their masculinity. Jesus possessed the traits of being strong and gentle. Women are capable of being assertive and independent while still keeping their femininity. Women can be leaders in the church as well as wives and mothers.

The God-ordained differences in females and males should be respected. The Creator created each sex with differences that complement each other. God designated the male to be head of the wife, but the husband must also follow God's marriage guidelines. Men, love your wives just as Jesus loves the church. Jesus never abused the church. Christians, we are the church.

Radical feminism is not acceptable in Christian marriages; neither is macho aggression. The key word is balance. Societal history shows that the pendulum swings from one extreme to the other; but doesn't stop in the middle, where balance is achieved.

<u>Passive slavery</u>
women viewed as possessions
women cannot vote or
  own property
women can be legally beaten
  by husbands
discrimination in the work force
victimized by a male dominant
  society
unequal educational opportunities

<u>Radical Feminism</u>
gender neutral
anti-male agendas
militant political agendas
women in combat
abortion rights
discrimination against males
critical view of homemakers

<u>Balance</u>
equality for our daughters and our sons
equal pay for equal work
equal educational opportunities

freedom to build careers
freedom to be homemakers

God is Spirit. God possesses both male and female traits. Jesus, the personhood of God, possessed both male and female traits while He walked this earth. The Bible says we will all be asexual in Heaven; neither male nor female bodies. (Matthew 22:30)

God is the creator of equality. Galatians 3:28 states, "There is neither Jew nor Greek, there is neither slave nor free man, there is neither *male nor female*; for you are all one in Christ Jesus." (Emphasis added)

Both victims and batterers use scripture passages to justify abusive behaviors:

Victims
- staying silent while husband abuses children
- obeying commands of sexual perversion
- being submissive to spiritual abuse
- staying silent in violent marriages
- accepting role of passive female
- saying, "The Bible says it's wrong to leave my husband for any reason."

Batterers
- twisting scriptures to demand abusive submission
- taking scriptures out of context
- believing wife and children are possessions
- justifying extreme physical abuse as punishment
- using violence to demand compliance
- accepting role of aggressive male
- saying, "The Bible says my wife should be submissive to me and obey my every command. I'm the head of the house and she should never question my authority."

God works within the cultural norms of a society. During the time of the Old Testament, men legally owned their wives and children. God did not condone family violence then, and He doesn't now. A fallen sinful world produces fallen sinful human beings who act in sinful ways. A fallen world produces imperfect laws and traditions. God never condoned the abuse of wives and children in the Old Testament. Battering men read the Old Testament and use the abuse of women to justify current domestic violence.

In the Old Testament, Moses allowed men to divorce their wives because of the hardness of men's hearts and for the protection of the innocent parties. (Matthew 19:7-8) God does not condone divorce, but He knows the imperfections of His creation. In the New Testament, Paul gives two exceptions to divorce. (1 Corinthians 7:1-40) The Bible states that God hates divorce. (Malachi 2:16) Which sin does God hate more—a husband beating his wife, or a physically abused wife divorcing her husband?

One reason spiritual abuse occurs is because many Christians do not have foundational knowledge of the Bible. They do not study the Bible. They listen to the preacher's sermon on Sunday and read their daily devotions, but remain ignorant of Bible history, culture, and doctrine. Many batterers and victims are educated professionals, but are still Bible illiterate.

There are ministers who preach the false doctrine of inequality between male and females. Whether this is due to ignorance, ego, or evil, only God may judge. These ministers advise and even demand the wives of their congregational members to stay in violent marriages. When the truth of the Bible is violated and discarded, sin and chaos are the results. Through the centuries, the church has been silent about domestic violence in Christian homes. This ideology is changing in our churches of today. The evidence of change is being seen in church-based counseling centers and support groups for male batterers. Sunday sermons and television evangelists are addressing family violence. Christian-based domestic violence shelters are springing up to minister to broken families.

In many churches, Bible studies are being replaced by church dinners, concerts, conferences, entertainment, and support groups. Readers, do not misunderstand the point. Church activities that promote fellowship in the body of Christ are necessary and appropriate; but church activities that usurp and take precedence over Bible studies hinder spiritual growth and diminish the effectiveness of the life changing-power of the Holy Spirit. The word of God is powerful. The Bible calls the word of God the sword of the Spirit. (Ephesians 6:17)

The Bible is the inherent word of God inspired by the Holy Spirit. The problem lies in the misinterpretation of the scripture verses by batterers and clergy who have not studied the actual meaning of the original word "submission" in the Greek language.

For further reading on the subject of biblical doctrine concerning the subjects of submission, headship, and the role of women in the Bible, I recommend, *Battered Into Submission*, by Phyllis and James Alsdurf. Citing their findings from extensive research and summarizing eight years of interviews with victims, abusers, and pastors, James and Phyllis provide a comprehensive approach to domestic violence in Christian homes.

> "Wife abuse is a problem we dare not ignore. We must learn how and why wife abuse occurs in Christian homes, and we must grasp what it is telling us about our view of marriage and male-female relationships. For there is trouble in paradise."[1]

For more information about the original meaning of the New Testament Greek word "hupotasso," which is used for "submission," read the chapter, "Let's Look at the Biblical Concept of Submission," by Catherine Clark Kroeger in *Violence Against Women and Children*.

> "The Bible has been cruelly misused in the hands of those who seek justification for abuse of women. Wife-abusers frequently insist that women are to "submit", but they give little regard to the actual meaning of the word in the New Testament. They argue for the validity of male headship, but do not ask what the concept meant to the original authors. We must be careful not to handle the text dishonestly."[2]

Scripture Verses

The following are popular scriptures that are misinterpreted and taken out of context by religious male batterers to justify domestic violence.

SUBMISSION

(These verses are used to justify physical, emotional, verbal, sexual, spiritual, economic, and parental-authority abuse if the wives object to any command or do not comply with unreasonable orders.)

Genesis 3:16
Yet your desire shall be for your husband, and he shall rule over you.

Ephesians 5:22, 24
Wives, be submissive to your own husbands, as to the Lord.
But as the church is subject to Christ, so also the wives ought to be to their husbands in everything.

1 Peter 3:1
In the same way, you wives, be submissive to your own husbands so that even if any of them are disobedient to the word, they may be won without a word by the behavior of their wives.

1 Timothy 2:11-12
Let a woman quietly receive instruction with entire submissiveness. But I do not allow a woman to teach or exercise authority over a man, but to remain quiet.

DIVORCE
(These verses are used if the wives try to seek help and attempt to leave if the abuse does not stop.)

Matthew 19:6 and Mark 10:9
What therefore God has joined together, let no man separate.

Mark 10:12
And if she herself divorces her husband and marries another, she is committing adultery.

Malachi 2:16
For I hate divorce, says the Lord, the God of Israel.

Romans 7:2-3
For the married woman is bound by law to her husband while he is living...So then if, while her husband is living, she is joined to another man, she shall be called an adulteress.

TEMPORARY SEPARATION FOR A SEASON
(This verse is used if the wife wants to temporarily separate until the abuser seeks counseling and learns to stop the physical violence.)

1 Corinthians 7:10
But to the married I give instruction, not I, but the Lord, that the wife should not leave her husband.

SEXUAL RELATIONS
(This verse is used to justify sex on demand and/or demeaning sexual acts or perversions.)

1 Corinthians 7:4-5
The wife does not have authority over her own body, but the husband does...Stop depriving one another, except by agreement for a time that you may devote yourselves to prayer.

TO CONTROL
(These verses are used to forbid wives to cut their hair, wear make-up, or wear certain articles of clothing. He denies her even small choices over her own body.)

1 Corinthians 11:15
But if a woman has long hair, it is a glory to her? For her hair is given to her for a covering.

1 Timothy 2:9
Likewise, I want women to adorn themselves with proper clothing, modestly and discreetly, not with braided hair and gold or pearls or costly garment.

To Victims of Domestic Violence:

It is imperative that you study the Bible about the true meanings of the above passages. Education, knowledge, information, and truth will empower you. God did not put these scriptures in the Bible for your husband to use to justify his abusive behaviors. The Bible contains the mind of God. The Bible does not condone domestic violence and it does not contradict itself.

Understanding the Bible

John 16:13 states, "But when He, the Spirit of truth comes, he will guide you into all truth..." Luke 24:45 states, "Then he opened their minds to understand the scriptures."

When reading, understanding, and interpreting the Bible, believers must have the presence of the Holy Spirit to guide them and illuminate the truth of God's word. Studying the Bible is not reserved for ministers and scholars only. Bible study is imperative for the spiritual knowledge and growth of all Christians. (Bible studying is more intense than simply reading the Bible.) Both batterers and victims must be taught correct theology in order that the oppression and perceived negative views of the female in religion as well as in society as a whole may ccase.

Basic Principles for Bible Study:
1. Determine the kind of literature
   - poetry   sermons   narratives   philosophy
   - history   instruction   letters   prophecy

2. Determine the context (i.e. the words or ideas that surround verses, and all verses before and after the passage you are interpreting in the chapter and book.)
   - Who wrote it?
   - To what audience was it written?
   - What is the major theme of the book and chapter?
   - Why was it written?
   - What subject is being discussed?
   - What is the meaning of the previous verse and preceding verse of the particular passage that is being interpreted?

3. Determine the historical background
   - Who wrote it?
   - Where was it written?
   - What was the culture like at this time?

4. Determine the grammatical meaning
   - What did the word or idea mean at the time it was expressed and written in Hebrew or Greek?
   - What part of speech is being used?

Bible dictionaries, commentaries, Bible handbooks, computer programs, and other resources are available to help us understand the meanings of words. These items can be purchased at your local Christian bookstore or found at a public library. Many churches have libraries for their members. You do not have to attend Bible college to learn how to study your Bible. Joining a Bible study group for women would greatly benefit victims of domestic violence, as long as the group leader taught correct doctrine and theology about the value of women to God.

The Value of Women to Jesus

The Bible is full of stories about women. God wanted these accounts of women in His word. The same Holy Spirit who hovered over the writings about men also hovered over the writings about women in order to bring truth into the world. Women and men need each other. There cannot be one without the other. Jesus was born into a patriarchal culture; hence the twelve disciples were all men. But Jesus still showed His love, respect, and purpose in the lives of Biblical women.

Dear Sisters in Christ,
   This section is written to encourage you to take another look at your value to God. I urge you to study upon the importance of women to Jesus. Ponder on the ways Jesus treated women in the Bible. You will learn a great deal from their suffering and sorrow as well as from their joy and happiness.

Women in the Old Testament:

Eve—a woman with great joy and great sorrow
(wife of Adam, and a mother)
God gave equally to Eve the gift of dominion to rule over the earth with Adam. (Genesis 1:26,28)

Sarah—a woman who showed great commitment
(wife of Abraham, and a mother)
God blessed a ninety-eight-year-old barren woman with a beautiful baby boy. (Genesis 11-23)

Jochebed—a woman with great wisdom
(mother of Moses)
God gave her great faith and wisdom by helping her to hide Moses from Pharaoh's decree to kill all male Hebrew babies. Her name signifies that Jehovah is her glory. (Exodus 1:2 and 1-11, Numbers 26:59)

Miriam—a woman of great leadership and courage
(daughter of Jochebed, sister to Moses)
She was a prophetess, the first female leader to Israel, and the first woman to sing on record in the Bible. She helped lead her people across the Red Sea. (Exodus 2:1-11, Numbers 12, Numbers 20:1, and Micah 6:4)

Hannah—a woman of great faith
(mother of the prophet Samuel)
Hannah prayed to God for a child, promised to give the child back to God, and she faithfully kept her word. Her son became a mighty man of God. (1 Samuel 25)

Deborah—a woman of great leadership
(early judge, prophetess, and wife of Lappidoth)
She won a great victory for God and Israel and showed her strength and ability as an inspirational leader. (Judges 4 and 5)

Ruth—a woman of great compassion
(daughter-in-law of Naomi)
Ruth is in the ancestral line of Jesus, and she even has an entire chapter named after her in the Bible. (Book of Ruth)

Queen Esther—a woman of great courage
(niece of Mordecai, wife of King Ahasucrus)
She helped to save Israel from destruction by being obedient to the Lord. She also has a Book of the Bible named after her. (Book of Esther)

Other worthy Biblical women given space in the Old Testament:

Rebekah	(Genesis 24, 25:20, 21, 28, and 26:7,8, 35:8-9, 27, 28)
Rachel and Leah	(Genesis 29-35)
Rahab	(Joshua 2-6)
Abigail	(1 Samuel 25)
Rizpah	(2 Samuel 21:1-15)

Women in the New Testament:

Mary—a woman greatly blessed
(wife of Joseph, mother of Jesus)
Mary was chosen by God to give birth to His son, Jesus. She was a godly mother and role model to Jesus and all who knew her. (Matthew 1,2, 26-28, Luke 1,2 John 19-21, and Acts 1,2)

Elizabeth—a woman of positive thinking
(wife of Zacharias, mother of John the Baptist, and cousin to Mary)
She was chosen by God to give birth to John. She was a woman of faith, discernment, and commitment. (Luke 1)

Mary and Martha—women of great hospitality
(sisters of Lazarus)
They opened their home to Jesus and fervently offered their servanthood. (Luke 10:38-42 and John 11)

Salome—a woman of assertiveness
(wife of Zebedee and mother to James and John, two of Jesus' disciples)
She was not afraid to speak her opinion. (Matthew 20:20-29 and Mark 16:1-9)

Mary of Magdala—a woman of great gratitude
Jesus healed her and delivered her from seven demons. She was the first person to see Jesus after His resurrection. (Matthew 27:56-62, 28:1, Mark 15:40-42, Luke 8:2, 24:8-13, and John 19:25, 20:1-19)

Lydia—a woman with a great mind for business
She was a successful businesswoman who held prayer meetings in her home. Her prestigious reputation did not hinder her from serving Jesus. (Acts 16)

Other worthy Biblical women given space in the New Testament:

Dorcas	(Acts 9:36-41)
Priscilla	(Acts 18)
Phoebe	(Romans 16:1-2)
Eunice and Lois	(2 Timothy 1:5)

[Adapted from *God Speaks to Women Today* (1964), Eugenia Price.]

True Story

Brenna and Alex attended church three times a week. Alex sang in the choir. Their marriage was a mess. They both carried emotional baggage from childhood and first marriages into their new life together. They prayed together, read the Bible together, and spent time taking care of their farm animals. They fought and cried together. Brenna was critical, controlling, and domineering. She would try to leave after starting a fight, but Alex would pin her down to make her stay. This pattern continued and escalated into physical violence by both parties. They desperately wanted and accepted Christian counseling. Alex was severely beaten by his father during childhood and Brenna had consistently witnessed her father and stepfather beating her mother. Both Alex and Brenna spent 30 days in a Christian psychiatric unit. After six months of intense counseling, their marriage was saved.

Chapter Five

Jesus Therapy

Jesus Therapy for Batterers

Jesus is our role model for healing broken people and broken relationships. The Bible is our recovery manual. The Holy Spirit is our change agent. Faith is our door. Pastors, counselors, and helpers are God's instruments. He uses us to pour out His compassion, encouragement, hope, love, and truth. Only Jesus can bring healing to the depths of our hearts. He created us. He knows how to heal us. He is the foundation of healthy people and healthy relationships. Batterers can change with the help of the Holy Spirit. The power of God's presence in our lives is underestimated. It is everything! Jesus offers:

- **Healing** for the past
- **Help** for the present
- **Hope** for the future

We cannot empty lives of violence without filling them with something else. That something else is the power of the Holy Spirit! Helping the batterer to KNOW Jesus is essential. This is Jesus Therapy in a nutshell! The question is—how do we help batterers to really know Jesus and to find their identity in Jesus? It's their choice. God will not force them to change. Desire can be used temporarily, but for permanent healing the power of Christ is essential. The desire to change is not enough. Jeremiah 17:9 states: "Our hearts are masters of denial and self-deception." If the batterer does not want to have a right relationship with Jesus, then permanent healing is hopeless. Only Christ-centered solutions will suffice.

Causes of Domestic Violence:

1. Original sin, generational curses, Satan and demons, strongholds, the spiritual battle, an uncontrolled spirit, and rebellion/separation from God. Luke 6:45 states: "The abuser speaks on what fills his heart."

2. Learned violence: past family abuse and generational domestic violence
3. Internal stress/external stress: feelings of insecurity, powerlessness, and fear of abandonment
4. Mental Disorders: clinical depression, post-traumatic stress disorder, personality disorders: narcissistic, antisocial, borderline, schizoid, and avoidant
5. Traditional view of women as less than equal: unequal power between males and females, societal and political mistreatment of women, negative view of women in religion and church history taught by religious professionals, pornography and television violence which demean women
6. Religious misogynists: men who hate women but still marry them
7. Severe head trauma which causes impulse-control problems[1]

The above reasons are not to be used as excuses for violent behaviors. Every adult is responsible for his/her behaviors to others.

PROBLEM: Denial and Blame
TREATMENT: Admit there is a problem
TOOLS: Confrontation from the pastor/helper; accept personal responsibility for his behaviors.
PRAYER: "Father, help me to walk in truth and light."
SCRIPTURES: Ephesians 5:13, Psalms 66:18
INTERCESSORY PRAYER: "Father, give _____ spiritual discernment to know your truth. Open his spiritual eyes. Help him to admit the problem to you. In Jesus' name."

The only problem you can solve is the problem you admit. Part of the process is to recognize and understand THE problem. People are not problems. People have problems. The reality of jail and separation from his family often makes denial impossible and forces the truth to surface.

Blame is a companion of denial. Batterers are masters of the blame game. They are experts at making excuses. Adam blamed Eve, who blamed the serpent. Both tried to justify their behavior of disobeying God.

God sent Nathan to King David to help the truth surface about the deception and murder of Uriah. David admitted to the murder as well as the adulterous affair with Bathsheba. God uses human messengers to speak the truth and confront the batterer. When the secret of family violence is revealed, the batterer loses his mask and his hiding place, and healing can begin. Leading a person to the truth about his/her problems is a step in the healing process.

PROBLEM: Deception, Sin, and Rebellion against God
TREATMENT: Confession and Repentance
TOOLS: Truth and the blood of Jesus; confrontation by the pastor/helper; accountability; give praise to God.
PRAYER: "Father, I ask for the power of the blood of Jesus to cleanse me from my lies."
SCRIPTURES: Acts 26:20, John 3:3, Galatians 5:16, Matthew 12:34, Colossians 3:15
INTERCESSORY PRAYER: "Father, by your redemption, I claim ____ for Christ because of the cross and shedding of blood. Bring unconfessed sin into the light and help him to submit and surrender to the Lordship of Christ. In Jesus' name."

Pathological lying and manipulation are weapons of the batterer. He tells one lie and two more are needed to cover it up. Unconfessed sin is a cancer on the soul. Untreated cancer continues to grow and spread until the entire body is destroyed. Unconfessed sin can destroy a personal relationship with the Holy Spirit. "A man who refuses to admit his mistakes can never be successful. But if he confesses and forsakes them, he gets another chance." (Proverbs 28:13, LB)

Sin is the root cause of domestic violence. Spiritual problems require spiritual solutions. Emotional and physical problems require spiritual solutions in addition to emotional and physical solutions. There is no single event we can point to—many events in life precede family violence.

The batterer is at war with God and with himself. Domestic violence is a sin against God. The inner battle spills out into his environment. He beats himself up on the inside as he beats his wife up on the outside. The spiritual crisis of battering men can be solved with a spiritual solution by a spiritual counselor operating as an instrument of a spiritual God. A cracked spiritual foundation needs to be rebuilt.

When a carpenter puts siding on a house, he covers up the old weathered boards underneath. Many batterers' spiritual experiences are like this example. They have not experienced a true conversion. The heart is more deceitful than all else and is desperately sick; who can understand it? (Jeremiah 17:9) A true conversion with the Holy Spirit makes the whole house new. God gives a new heart. He doesn't patch up the old heart. God specializes in heart transplants. The heart must be baptized in the Holy Spirit. As a new creation, the Holy Spirit can help the person to heal past hurts through a process of inner healing and a renewing of the mind. The human flesh can be brought under the power of submission. Brokenness comes before transformation. Sometimes it is only when we are lying on the ground looking up that we gain a new perspective of Who God is.

The power of the blood of Jesus is the solution for the cleansing of the soul. Satan will flee as we speak the blood of Jesus. Deliverance from the power of the sin of wife beating is necessary. God will work in a man's spirit to renew his soul and body. 1 Thessalonians 5:23 reads: "Now may the God of peace Himself sanctify you entirely; and may your spirit and soul and body be preserved complete, without blame at the coming of our Lord Jesus Christ."

The power of confession is life changing. Confession is a spiritual antiseptic to the soul. A doctor cleans out a wound before healing, so it will not become infected. The antiseptic is painful but necessary.

Helpers need to speak God's truth in love. God's truth will expose Satan's lie. The truth will break Satan's power. The truth will set you free. (John 8:32) Any truth is God's truth, as God is the author. Megadoses of truth can transform us if we choose to listen with our spirits. The truth never changes—we change. We can run away from the truth, but when we return, the truth will still be there where we left it. People who have secrets will be haunted by the truth. Pastors, counselors, and helpers can offer intercessory prayer, encouragement, listening, confrontation, teaching of coping skills, education, and point the way to the Great Physician—but only God can heal. Doctors can treat, prescribe medication, set fractured bones, perform surgery on all parts of the body, deliver babies, and do organ transplants, but only God can heal.

PROBLEM: Learned Family Violence
TREATMENT: Unlearn family violence
TOOLS: Christian support group for batterers; genograph; education on family patterns.
PRAYER: "Father, help me to break the cycle of abuse to my wife and children."
SCRIPTURES: Proverbs 16:29, Ezekiel 7:23, Isaiah 60:18, Matthew 26:52
INTERCESSORY PRAYER: "Father, help ____ to unlearn his past violent behaviors. I pray he would never again use his fists to assault his wife or children. Help him to root out his anger. Jesus, be his role model. In Jesus' name."

Domestic violence is not a disease. It is learned behaviors. We produce what we are. Children model the behaviors they see with their eyes and the words they hear with their ears. They model the words that come from their parents' lips. Children learn distorted thinking.

Violent tempers are not inherited—violent tempers are learned. Children learn to hit, slap, kick, and physically assault others.

What is the pay-off of physical abuse? It works quickly! People will do what you want them to do out of fear. Fear of pain is a motivator to do exactly what the abuser demands. Hurting people hurt other people. What purpose does the violence serve in the abuser's life? He gets what he wants and he gets it now! Men who were abused in childhood are often wounded children in adult bodies. Pain and suffering do not originate with only one event in life. They are the result of many lifetime events. Educating a batterer about generational violence helps him to understand how he became an abuser. This process is not used to blame his parents or caretakers, nor is it used to give him excuses for his violent behaviors. Giving knowledge is a tool to understanding, changing, and empowerment. The past does not have to be your own private prison.

It helps to teach batterers to separate their behaviors from their identities. By doing this we can judge the behaviors as right or wrong, or good or bad, without judging the value of the person. People have problems—people are not problems.

Abusers need to learn how to set physical boundaries. To respect oneself is to respect others. Wives and children are not personal property.

The myth needs to be dispelled. Victims do not like to be beaten and they do not encourage it. The helper and members of the Christian support group must challenge the attitude of macho male authority. Batterers must give up their weapons during treatment (guns, knives, etc.)

The process of family restoration will take approximately six to eighteen months, depending on several factors. The abuser needs to prove himself before he is returned to the home. Do not rush this process! Safety is still the number one issue for the wife and children.

A person's perception of a situation helps or hinders the healing process. For example, if three people were standing on a street corner and witnessed a car accident:

- Witness #1 may state that the red car hit the blue car.
- Witness #2 may state that the blue car hit the red car.
- Witness #3 may state that the two cars hit each other at the same time.

All three witnesses believe in their version of the truth. The two drivers of the cars also have two different perceptions of the accident.

Perceptions are based on how we see the world and what colored our world during childhood. God's word is always the truth. God's word says abuse is wrong.

PROBLEM: Generational Curses, Demons, Spiritual Warfare, and Ungodly Strongholds
TREATMENT: Teach the full armor of God (Ephesians 6:11-22); build Godly strongholds.
TOOLS: Prayer, Bible, accountability partner, fasting, church attendance, and deliverance.
PRAYER: "Father, protect me in the spiritual warfare and help me to break the cycle of violence in my home. Remove the evil presence of the forces of darkness. I pull down the stronghold of _____ by the power and authority of the blood of Jesus Christ."
SCRIPTURES: 2 Corinthians 10:4-5, Luke 10:17-19, Matthew 18:18
INTERCESSORY PRAYER: "Father, Holy Spirit, reveal any strongholds which give the demons ground to oppress and afflict this believer. Release him from bondage by the authority of Jesus Christ. I break every demonic curse placed on him from the womb to the tomb. In the power of Jesus' name."

Exodus states that the sins of the fathers are passed down to the children. Sin multiplies. Children and grandchildren often take the sins of their parents to a higher level. Unchecked sin increases from generation to generation. A husband beats his wife. His son becomes a murderer. Adam and Eve disobeyed God. Their son killed his brother Abel. (Genesis 4:5-8) Generational curses must be broken by the authority of Jesus.

Satan hates God's children, and he hates the institution of marriage. Why? Because God created people and marriage. Satan will do anything to destroy Christian families.

Satan uses the same tactics today as he used in the Garden of Eden. He lied then and he lies now. He uses the same methods he used when he battled Jesus for forty days in the wilderness. He twists the words of God and misquotes scripture.

Strongholds are areas of human weakness that function as the access point of sin. (Ephesians 4:26,27) Strongholds not rooted out can control the person and put him in a state of habitual sin. Strongholds have a root of bitterness that enslaves the person. (Hebrews 12:15)

The Bible gives a description of the strongman in Matthew 12:22,28. Warfare praying will break the strongman (Satan). (James

4:7,8 and 1 Peter 5:8-11) The Holy Spirit within us is a force greater than Satan and his demons. A batterer can possess a spirit of control. The Bible states that demons bind and oppress men. (Matthew 12:22-29, Luke 13:10-16, Revelation 12:4-7)

Examples of ungodly strongholds (they can be anything that puts you in a state of bondage):

pride	greed	unbelief	jealousy
fear	bitterness	selfishness	unforgiving
suspicion	insecurities	prejudices	dishonesty
judgmental	criticism	hatred of self	false doctrine
resentment	paranoia	self-righteousness	rejection
lust	bad attitude	wrong thinking	addictions

Take the opposite of the above ungodly strongholds and seek repentance, healing, and deliverance by the power of Jesus Christ, then put the Godly strongholds into practice in every area of your life.

PROBLEM: Wrong Thinking
TREATMENT: Right thinking and logical reasoning
TOOLS: Bible scriptures to renew the mind and identify negative thinking patterns and negative self-talk, replacing them with positive self-talk
PRAYER: "Father, please renew my mind as I study on Your word."
SCRIPTURES: See section on Tools for Counseling for a list of scriptures.
INTERCESSORY PRAYER: "Father, lead ____ to repentance by the conviction of his conscience. Cleanse his mind by the power of your word and the blood of Christ. Holy Spirit, who dwells within him, bring his past memories of pain into the light of Jesus for healing. In Jesus' name."

We can master our thought processes. It is easy? No. Is it possible? Yes. God has given us several scriptures in the New Testament to meditate on to renew our minds. We need to memorize these verses and recite them out loud daily. Life is a process of learning, unlearning, and relearning.

Once we master our thoughts, we can master our behaviors more easily. A thought precedes a behavior. You need to change the inside before you change the outside. Sin is manifested in the thought before being acted out in the deed. God created our brains. He knows what our brains need to be reprogrammed. The area of Christian counseling that addresses the healing of repressed and suppressed memories is appropriate.

One evangelist says he prays out loud for the salvation of a particular unsaved person every time an unclean, immoral thought tempts him. He believes if this person gets saved, Satan will think twice before putting negative, lustful thoughts into his head again.

Abusive men have black or white thinking. "I am right, and you are wrong." Their responses are judgmental and critical. Humans are creatures of habit. We can make a conscious effort to break old destructive patterns of negative thinking. We replace "stinkin' thinkin'" with positive thinking. It takes time to permanently break old habits, but with God all things are possible. The first step is to be aware of our negative thoughts and to interrupt them. Next, we can counteract them with positive words. The words of God are powerful and positive.

Our mental faculties consist of our intellect, will, emotions, ego, and conscience, which are all housed in the brain. Teach the batterer to test his cognitive processes.

Mental Faculty	Question to Ask
emotion	What do I feel?
intellect	Is what I am thinking reasonable and biblical?
will	What is my intent? Why do I want to do it?
ego	What is my motive?
conscience	Is it right or wrong, according to God's standards?

PROBLEM: A Weak Conscience
TREATMENT: Conviction of the Holy Spirit
TOOLS: Scripture and Confrontation
PRAYER: "Father, convict my conscience when I disobey and do wrong. Renew a right spirit within me."
SCRIPTURES: See below
INTERCESSORY PRAYER: "Father, speak to his conscience through your Holy Spirit. Remove the layers that cover up his sin and his inability to hear your voice. In Jesus' name."

What does the Bible say about the conscience?
- Holy Spirit influences us through our conscience (Romans 9:1)
- a weak conscience (1 Corinthians 8:7)
- a defiled conscience (Titus 1:15)

- a conscience seared with a hot iron (2 Corinthians 1:12)
- a conscience void of offense (Acts 24:16)
- a pure conscience (1 Timothy 3:9)
- a good conscience (Acts 23:1 and Hebrews 13:18)
- a good conscience towards God (1 Peter 3:21)

The batterer is experiencing problems with his conscience. He ignores the Holy Spirit when he abuses his wife, or he does not have a relationship with the Holy Spirit.

PROBLEM: Appetite for Power and Control
TREATMENT: Empowerment through the Holy Spirit and surrender to God
TOOLS: Obedience, education and the power of our choices
PRAYER: "Father, take away my craving for power and replace it with Holy Spirit power."
SCRIPTURES: John 3:30, Hebrews 5:8, Galatians 6:3
INTERCESSORY PRAYER: "Father, tear down the strongholds of resentment and bitterness. Help ____ to surrender to your authority. Deliver him from the spirit of control that has taken him captive. In the power of the name of Jesus."

Power can be used for good or evil. Power itself is neutral. God uses power for good, and Satan uses power for evil. As humans, we have the choice to use power for good or for evil.

Why do these men crave power and control? An abused, powerless child will turn into an adult who uses power to control others. He finally feels in control when he is making others do what he wants them to do. He is also seeking revenge against his past abusers. This behavior may be conscious or subconscious. The Bible states: "for by what a man is overcome, by this he is enslaved." (2 Peter 2:19b) A batterer is enslaved to his violent anger. He returns to it like a dog returns to its own vomit. (2 Peter 2:22) Power becomes the idol he worships. The batterer, who so desperately desires power and control, has become a slave to evil and, hence, powerless.

Batterers use:
- power without compassion
- authority without humbleness
- anger without self-control
- pleasure without conscience
- punishment without justice or mercy

The batterer needs to be taught about the biblical balance of power. God designed men to be:

    Head of the wife—but in equal submission with his wife. (Ephesians 5:21)

    Spiritual leader of the home—but in submission to his headship, Jesus Christ. (Ephesians 4:15)

    Provider for his family—a protector. (Ephesians 5:28-29)

He needs to be taught the Biblical truth about how God wants him to treat his wife. He cannot take scripture out of context and use it as a weapon to control his wife and children. A male pastor with correct theology would be a positive role model for the batterer.

Abraham Lincoln stated, "I discovered I always have choices, and sometimes it's only a choice of attitude." Learning that we choose our attitudes is an empowering concept. Learning that we choose our reactions can be puzzling. Learning that we allow ourselves to become angry and that nobody makes us angry without our permission is a difficult lesson. We do have power when we choose how we want to respond to others. We make hundreds of decisions daily by reacting to what others do.

There is legitimate power. Parents have the power to make their children clean their rooms. They either reward or punish them. Obeying the laws of our land is a legitimate use of power. Without legitimate power, the world would be in a state of chaos. George Bush once stated, "Use power to help people. For we are given power not to advance our own purposes nor to make a great show in the world, nor a name. There is but one just use of power, and it is to serve people."

Christians know God is in control and is all-powerful. We take comfort in His power, unless we have a distorted view of Him. If we do not have a personal relationship with God, we will resent His power and view Him as a mean old tyrant; just waiting to strike us down for our mistakes. We will see His justice but miss His mercy.

PROBLEM: Emotions Out of Balance
TREATMENT: Holy Spirit control and education about emotions
TOOLS: Holy Spirit test, behavior contracts, red flags, and faith
PRAYER: Father, help me to know your Holy Spirit."
SCRIPTURES: Proverbs 25:28, Romans 7:223, Titus 1:7-8
INTERCESSORY PRAYER: "Father, fill ____ with the Spirit of God. Give him love, joy, peace, and self-control. In Jesus' name."

God is the author of our emotions. Jesus received the same human emotions that we received in creation. Emotions are like a ride on a roller-coaster, up-and-down and up-and down continuously. Emotions are neutral, neither good or bad. Emotions give us energy for our lives. Emotions are God's gauges to let you know what is going on inside of you. Humans can learn to respond to their emotional gauges. The level of intensity of our emotions is our warning signal that something may explode if we don't check ourselves. Pay attention to your feelings. Don't ignore feelings—explore feelings. Our response is a test of the Holy Spirit. If we have a personal relationship with the Holy Spirit, He will help us to respond without hurting others. This relationship, like any relationship, takes time to grow and must be nurtured.

Often feelings cannot be trusted. Our feelings can lie to us. Feelings fluctuate. It is not what you feel, it is what you know. What we are like under pressure is what we are like. If you know God's word, you know He can be trusted. The symptoms of chest pain, tingling in the left arm, and shortness of breath are signs of a physical heart attack. The symptoms of violent anger, rage, and bitterness are signs of an emotional heart attack. A person with a wounded heart, attacks others. "A fool expresses all his emotions, but a wise person controls them." (Proverbs 29:11, LB)

A battering man can learn to use the "red flag" concept. When he feels an emotion intensifying, he needs to walk away from the situation, identify the emotion, and think about what he needs to do to express himself in a nonviolent way. This technique should not be used to avoid problems.

Americans have bought into the "feel-good-all-the-time" myth. We alter our moods when we feel grief, fear, sadness, or sorrow. We use alcohol, drugs, sex, violence, recreation, gambling, spending money on shopping sprees, or whatever it takes to escape from unhappy emotions. Temporary suffering is a part of human existence, so we need to teach batterers and victims how to deal with emotional pain and how to seek help. People who commit suicide do not want to die, they just want the pain to go away; but they do not know how to help themselves. Learning God's truth about our emotions will set us free psychologically.

Our beliefs can determine how we feel. We can evoke certain emotions by what we tell ourselves. The emotions that flow through our bodies can become unbalanced. We can experience a continual flood of emotions, which puts us in a state of constant anxiety. We can also experience a severe drought of emotions, which puts us in a state of numbness.

As Christians, we can walk by faith instead of by feelings. For example, if a caboose on the end of the trains represents our feelings, and the train represents our thinking area; we often allow the caboose to get ahead of our train. Our caboose (feelings) can run away from the train (our thinking). Repeat this phrase to yourself" "My feelings go up and down. I can't trust my feelings today, but I can trust what I know from God's word. I will walk by faith today, even if I feel like an emotional sewer. God will help me to get through this valley."

PROBLEM: Violent Anger
TREATMENT: Self-control and accepting sole responsibility for anger
TOOLS: Holy Spirit, fasting, anger management, the legal system, male support group for Christian batterers, individual counseling; ask the question: "What would Jesus do if He were angry?"
PRAYER: "Father, help me to understand my anger. Help me never to use my hands to hurt my wife and children."
SCRIPTURES: Ephesians 4:26-27, see section on Batterer to Believer for a list of scriptures on anger.
INTERCESSORY PRAYER: "Father, apply the outcome of your resurrection to create a new heart in ____. Let the power of the Holy Spirit help him control his violent anger. Cleanse him from his old nature. Help him walk in the spirit and not his flesh. Help him to submit his mind, will, and emotions to you. In Jesus' name."

Teaching batterers anger management skills is only part of the process. Batterers continuously use power and control techniques, even when they are not angry. Anger does not cause battering. Treating their wives with kindness during the honeymoon stage is a product of manipulation and control, with the purpose of assuring spousal compliance. However, anger does exacerbate violence.

There are no easy techniques to help a violent batterer learn to control his deadly anger and rage. Please listen—the power of the Holy Spirit is the ONLY way to help a Christian batterer to change his violent behaviors! Teaching anger management skills alone is nothing more than putting a Band-Aid on a gushing wound. Our reactions show either an abundance or a lack of Holy Spirit relationship.

Battering men can be compared to volcanoes. There is a reservoir of lava (anger) under the surface just waiting to erupt and spew destruction on the innocent people in his path. The pressure inside builds and builds, until finally his rage explodes.

Anger is a normal emotion created by God. The Bible says God gets angry at times. Jesus became angry when he went into the temple and saw how the religious leaders were financially cheating the Jewish people. There are many examples in the Bible in which God's people experienced anger. Anger is part of the package that comes with being a human creation. The emotion of anger is not good or bad. It just is. God gave us the emotion of anger for a purpose.

Anger is an essential ingredient in motivating and energizing us to perform great and mighty deeds for justice. Before coming to Christ, Paul used his anger to hunt and kill Christians. After his conversion, he used his anger to fight Satan and sin in the churches. It was the same emotion—first Paul used his anger for evil, then he used it for good. The ability to express anger in a healthy way is part of being a healthy person.

Anger produces a reaction in the physical body. The heart beats faster and blood pressure increases. Additional adrenaline is released. Breathing rate increases. Muscles tense up. The body is reacting to thoughts and emotions. Anger is a powerful emotion.

The reactions to angry emotions are learned in childhood. If a child is taught not to show anger, he/she will repress it. This anger has to go somewhere. Anger turned inward will cause depression. If parents react to anger with blaming, yelling, or physical violence, then the child will model this behavior. The emotion of anger makes an adult feel powerful and in control. Negative anger blocks the flow of the positive emotions of love and joy.

A batterer is full of anger. His anger turns into rage. Rage spills over into his behavior. He hits, pushes, and hurts others. A batterer does have control. When he is angry, does he hit the boss? No. He knows the boss will fire him or have him arrested. Does he hit the cashier at the gas station for being too slow? No. He knows the consequences. Who does he hit? His wife and children. Why? He knows they will not hit back or call the police to arrest him. But yet, he pleads no self-control. He uses anger first as a tool to abuse, and then as an excuse.

Batterers possess old anger. Anger left unresolved or buried will take root and grow seeds of bitterness and resentment. The leaves of a tree show the condition of the roots. The expressed emotions show the condition of the heart. The batterer carries an interior suitcase full of past hurts and emotional garbage.

What is at the root cause of the batterer's anger?
- The emotions of hurt, fear, sadness, confusion, and perceived mistreatment
- Feelings of betrayal, rejection, and abandonment by others in his life
- Feelings of being powerless and not in control
- Unconfessed sin and hatred of self
- Past childhood sexual, physical, emotional, verbal, and spiritually abuse
- Selfishness and an uncontrolled spirit

Lies from Satan about anger:
- I have a bad temper, and I can't control it.
- People make me mad, and it's their fault.
- I have every right to get angry when I don't get what I deserve.
- I'm the head of this family, and you need to obey my commands without question!

What are the symptoms on the surface? He expresses anxiety, frustration, aggression, depression, stress, confusion, anger, rage, resentment, and bitterness. He blames his family, his boss, and society for all his problems. "Don't point your finger at someone else and try to pass the blame!" (Hosea 4:4, NLT) How do I help the batterer change? Help him:

Admit and confess the anger that motivated him to inflict pain on his family. Confess it, don't repress it, suppress it, or express it in violent ways. Who and what is the batterer beating when he takes anger out on his wife and children?

Ask for a cleansing by the Holy Spirit. (Galatians 5:22-23)

Learn the consequences of his violent behavior. (Romans 6:23)
- Jail—the ultimate consequence
- Separation from his family, either temporarily or permanently.

Learn to accept sole responsibility for his violent behaviors.
We create our own anger. Nobody makes us. It is our fault. We have to change.

Recognize physical body cues, reactions, and triggers.
- Deep breathing exercises (practice this technique daily for 30 days)
- Make a crisis plan for explosive anger:

- Leave immediately and walk two or more miles, or allow his wife to leave
- See daily formula

Teaching a batterer to punch a pillow is not anger management. Teaching him to channel his anger energy through playing basketball, sports, or exercise is appropriate for a short-term behavioral goal. Teaching him to change his triggers and negative thought patterns is a long-term cognitive goal. Both short-term and long-term counseling goals for anger management are necessary.

Anger is the hardest emotion to learn to change and control in our lives. Why? Because anger is the quickest way to get what we want from others. Selfishness is a companion to anger. Anger multiplies and expands. Anger is contagious. Batterers carry around old anger, or rather they carry around the memories of past pain. A memory of a past hurtful experience is tied to the memory of the past painful emotion. When the memory surfaces, the same emotion surfaces, and the person recreates the same anger. Why did this past memory trigger the emotion of anger? Because the painful event has not been resolved, discussed, and healed. Painful memories from our past influence our present behaviors. When we tell a story of how someone wronged us, we continue to fuel our anger. Every time we tell this story, we feel the same anger over and over again. When we think about the injustice, our minds connect it to our emotions. Our minds are powerful. They believe what we tell them.

Jesus tells us to renew our minds. When we look at the past and untie the hurtful memory from the hurtful anger, we will cease to become angry every time the memory comes to the surface. Satan often throws our sins from the past (confessed-under-the-blood sins) in our faces to make us feel depressed, unworthy, and guilty. God puts our confessed sins as far as the East is from the West.

Battering men need to process their past painful memories and attach new emotions to them. Human beings will not forget their past abuse, but they can heal and learn to live a healthy, positive life. The key to healing is forgiveness. Giving the gift of understanding, hope, education, and insight can help a batterer to dissolve the anger associated with the past painful memories.

Many painful memories lie in our subconscious mind. We may be unaware of them, but they are like old garbage, stinking up our thinking, emotions, and behaviors. The Holy Spirit can bring what is in the darkness into the light. God created the part of our mind that is subconscious. He knows how to heal these memories. With the Holy Spirit as our guide, we, the helpers, can guide the process of "memory healing." The counselor/pastor is the intercessor. Ask the Holy Spirit to reveal the memories. The timing of the Holy Spirit is perfect; He will bring the memory to light when the counselee is ready to accept the truth. God wants the past to be forgiven, which brings permanent healing. Taking out one trash can full of garbage and leaving the rest will still smell up your house. Ignoring the garbage will still smell up your house. Pretending your garbage does not exist will smell up your house. Blaming someone else for not taking out your garbage will still smell up your house. You have to remove the garbage from your own house. Eventually, the garbage will draw bugs and rodents—flies, maggots, roaches, gnats, mice, and rats. Our minds are like reservoirs; storing up whatever we put into them. Garbage in = garbage out. Anger in = anger out. Resentment in = resentment out. Bitterness in = bitterness out. Forgiveness in = forgiveness out. God's love in = God's love out. Self-control in = self-control out. Joy in = joy out.

Our choices are a spiritual battleground. Satan fights to influence us to choose the wrong response. There are circumstances that will influence our choices, but we are solely responsible for how we respond and react as adults.

Many people believe that forgiving our abusers lets them (the abusers) off the hook. Some victims want revenge for their pain and sorrow. Forgiving our abusers will heal us—not them. Forgiveness does not condone the behaviors of the abusers. Abusers still deserve the earthly consequences of prison and possible loss of their families for their crimes. In God's plan, forgiveness is one of our solutions. God created us. He knows how to heal us.

The hardest situation for a wife to forgive is when her husband continues assaulting her over and over again. He asks for forgiveness and then he assaults her again. Forgiving the abuser does not mean she has to allow him back into the home to prove her Christianity. We can forgive others and choose not to have a future relationship with them. It is easier to forgive someone when they stop doing what they're doing. Holding on to unforgiveness from past abuse allows the abuser to indirectly still control the victim.

One married couple in therapy found that the only solution for them was to recognize their body cues and then immediately drop to their knees and pray out loud for God to intervene. Eventually they both spent thirty days at a Christian psychiatric ward, where they learned the root causes of their violent behaviors. Both the husband and wife were physically abusive to each other. The wife was an adult child of an alcoholic father and had witnessed her mother being beaten by her father and stepfather. The husband's father had abandoned the family in his childhood. Both were on their second marriages. They both attended church every Sunday before and after counseling. They spent approximately nine months in counseling before the process of change was completed. It takes time for batterers to change their violent behaviors. Even after they stop the physical abuse, the emotional and verbal abuse often continue.

Anger is a "safe" emotion for a batterer. The emotions of fear or sadness would produce a feeling he perceives as weakness. He doesn't want to appear weak. He wants to appear strong and powerful. "A fool gives full vent to his anger, but a wise man keeps himself under control." (Proverbs 29:11) A hot-tempered man...gets into all kinds of trouble." (Proverbs 29:22)

The batterer eventually alienates his wife and children. The end result of untreated violent anger is the loss of his family. If the family stays, they become apathetic and depressed. "The fool who provokes his family to anger and resentment will finally have nothing worthwhile left." (Proverbs 11:29)

PROBLEM: Inability to Love and Pathological Jealousy
TREATMENT: The Cross
TOOLS: Unconditional love of Christ; practice loving self and others; list twenty-five things you are thankful for in your life.
PRAYER: "Father, help me love You, love myself, and love others through the power of faith."
SCRIPTURES: Galatians 5:20, Ephesians 5:28-29, Colossians 3:19
INTERCESSORY PRAYER: "Father, increase the faith of ___. Help him to read your Word daily. Teach him to pray and talk to You. Show him Your great love; a love so great, You sent Your son to die on the cross. In Jesus' name."

Batterers do not love themselves. They possess narcissistic thoughts and behaviors, but they do not truly love themselves. Batterers are self-destructive. They have no clue as to what Godly love is all about—a love manifested only by the Holy Spirit working inward to help us express outward love to others.

A batterer has feelings for his family, but feelings come and go. He uses anger as a defense shield to avoid intimacy. His emotions have a way of short-circuiting when he allows himself to become angry and violent. As a child a batterer was slugged—not hugged. He was rejected, not accepted, by his caretakers. He can learn to love God, himself, and his family. It will take time.

Jealousy is the fear of losing what we have. Batterers hold so tightly that wives suffer from emotional suffocation. One wife's husband accused her of having an affair for fifteen years. He would not give up this fabrication. This husband had been unfaithful in his first marriage. The wife, who was innocent, lived for fifteen years with resentment for being falsely accused.

PROBLEM: Childhood Sexual Abuse
TREATMENT: Counseling, and processing childhood memories and pain.
TOOLS: A licensed, professional Christian psychologist or counselor, and Holy Spirit guidance
PRAYER: "Father, help the child in me to heal from sexual abuse."
SCRIPTURES: Psalm 147:3, Romans 8:37
INTERCESSORY PRAYER: "Jehovah Rapha, our God of healing, love and comfort ____. Heal the pain, terror, and memories of the past abuse. Show him your awesome compassion. Dry his tears of suffering. In Jesus' name."

The person needs to know that a sexual offense committed against him as a child is not his fault. They carry no blame. God hates sexual abuse against children. Many men keep the secret of child sexual abuse hidden. They use alcohol and/or drugs to escape the painful memories. As adults, these men try to prove their heterosexuality by forcing excessive sexual intercourse upon their spouses. The development of sexual addictions is common for this population.

Memories of childhood sexual abuse may be repressed or suppressed. Subconscious memories will be manifested in negative external behaviors. For example, an adult male with suppressed memories of sexual abuse may believe he is a homosexual. He denies this belief by demanding sexual compliance from his wife to all his sexual perversions. He may develop psychological impotence to avoid sexual relations.

The Holy Spirit takes a person back to where the problem originated by bringing the memories to the conscious mind. "Memory healing" must be used under the guidance of the Holy Spirit. Spiritual discernment on the part of the counselor is essential. Helpers can pray for the healing of the sins committed against the person when he/she was a child.

God created sex for procreation and for the pleasure of a man and a woman within the institution of marriage. The batterer has developed a distorted view of sex. Teach him a positive view of sex.

PROBLEM: Addiction to Pornography
TREATMENT: Cleansing and renewing of the mind
TOOLS: Accountability partner, behavior contracts, scriptures on temptation
PRAYER: "Father, give me the desire and courage to stop buying and exposing my mind to pornography. I claim deliverance from the love of my flesh."
SCRIPTURES: Ephesians 2:3, Romans 7:15, Romans 12:2, Job 31:1,4
INTERCESSORY PRAYER: "Father, deliver ____ from the attacks of lust and Satan. Show his weakness so he may become strong in you. Help him to fight temptation in your strength. Break the bondage of Satan's power by your blood. In Jesus' name."

Some Christian batterers suffer with a pornography addiction and admit it started in childhood. Their habit has continued for years, sometimes in secret and sometimes out in the open. The addiction often escalates to include calling sex hot-line numbers, affairs, and paying for prostitutes. Pornography feeds the myth that women deserve to be treated as objects, not as valuable human beings.

Satan uses pornography to increase our natural sexual feelings. The emotion turns into lust and the seeking of physical pleasure at any cost. All Christians have "temptation-buttons," but we allow Satan to push our buttons when we dwell on lustful thoughts and then put the thoughts into action.

PROBLEM: Inaccurate View of God the Father
TREATMENT: Explore earthly view of biological father or stepfather
TOOLS: Read the book, *The Blessing*, by Trent and Smalley
PRAYER: "Father, help me to see you as a loving Father."
SCRIPTURES: Galatians 4:6-7, Romans 6:15, James 4:8
INTERCESSORY PRAYER: "Abba, Father, help ____ to know and to feel your unconditional love and acceptance. Assure him you will never leave or forsake him. You are not his earthly father, you are his Heavenly Father. In Jesus' name."

Ask the person, "How would you describe God?" He will describe the attributes of his earthly father or stepfather. If he did not have a father or stepfather, he will describe God as distant and uncaring. What kind of painful memories does the word "father" evoke? Our view of our earthly father will determine our view of our Heavenly Father. The way you see God will determine how you see yourself.

What God does the batterer serve? He serves a God who is a composite of all the people who have hurt him. The God he serves is cold, unlovable, and unfair. He doesn't serve the God of the Bible. Satan is the accuser, not God. Often the batterer is so angry with God that he doesn't fear the judgment day. He feels justified in his anger towards God.

Teach the truth about God the Father:
- God is a compassionate Father. (Psalm 145:9 and Lamentations 3:22, NIV)
- God is a consistent Father. (Romans 11:29, LB)
- God does not lie. (Romans 11:29, LB)
- God will never stop loving me. (Psalm 59:10, LB)

Thoughts and behaviors are directly correlated to our spiritual relationship with the Heavenly Father. What you think and do affects your intimate connection to the Holy Spirit and connects you emotionally to Jesus. A believer can become disconnected through sin and will experience spiritual dryness, restlessness, confusion, sadness, and depression. How does a believer reconnect to Jesus?:
- admit you were wrong and Jesus was right
- accept His mercy and forgiveness
- apologize to the people you hurt
- analyze why you became disconnected
- avoid making the same mistakes again
- act with the right motives in the future
- activate a system of total honesty with yourself

PROBLEM: Alcohol and/or Drugs and Addictions
TREATMENT: Christian AA Meetings/Chemical Dependency Unit/medication
TOOLS: 12-Step Christian program and Christian support/treatment/education group for male abusers

PRAYER: "Father, I have the disease of alcoholism. Help me to stay sober. With the authority of the name of Jesus, I claim deliverance from alcohol and drugs."

SCRIPTURES: Psalm 103:2-3, Proverbs 4:17; Galatians 5:21

INTERCESSORY PRAYER: "Father, you placed the sins of ____ on the cross. Jesus' blood is the propitiation for his sins. I break the addiction of alcohol and drugs by the authority of Lord Jesus who defeated all rulers of darkness. Cover him with your protection. Keep him safe from temptation. In Jesus' name."

Alcohol is involved in:
- 60% of all child abuse cases
- 50% of all spouse abuse cases
- 40% of family court cases
- 50% of all violent deaths
- 70% of all murders
- 83% of all offenders in prison report alcohol was involved in their crimes.

(Chemical People Newsletter)

Alcohol and drugs are used to escape the pain of reality and to numb the memory of past pain. The batterer may possess an addictive personality. Other addictions include sex, television, sports, food, money, power, or any activity that becomes an unhealthy obsession. Addictions draw attention away from the real problems. Addictions are symptoms of the real problems.

An alcoholic batterer may benefit from a Chemical Dependency Unit or a day treatment program. Check the available community resources and his health insurance policy. Accompany him to Alcoholics Anonymous Meetings (AA) or Narcotics Anonymous (NA). Find AA and NA meetings where the higher power is Jesus Christ.

Do not allow him to use the excuse that alcohol or drug abuse "makes" him assault his wife. Alcohol and drug usage may increase the severity of the abuse, but they do not cause it. This statement is a cop-out. He chooses to drink or do drugs. Alcoholism is a sin first, and a disease second, for the Christian. There is an eighty-percent correlation between alcohol/drugs and domestic violence, but it is not the alcohol or drugs that cause the abuse. There are men who batter who do not use chemicals.

Alcohol and drugs will not fill emotional and spiritual emptiness. There is a vacuum inside of each person that only Christ can fill. That deep feeling of restlessness is a longing for our spirits to be reconciled with God. The solution is not outside of us. The solution is inside of us. The solution is a relationship with God's Holy Spirit. Nothing earthly will satisfy but Jesus. Instead of trying to medicate our emotional and spiritual aches and pain with chemical substances, we can turn to the care of the Holy Spirit. We will become less dependent on chemicals to make us feel better, and more dependent upon God.

PROBLEM: Unforgiveness
TREATMENT: Forgiveness, humbleness, amazing grace, and mercy
TOOLS: Scriptures on forgiveness
PRAYER: "Father, please forgive me. Help me to forgive others, and help my family to forgive me. Take away arrogance and replace it with humility."
SCRIPTURES: Luke 23:34, Romans 12:19, Matthew 6:14-15, Colossians 3:12-13
INTERCESSORY PRAYER: "Father, help ____ to stand on the power of the crucifixion and the victory of the resurrection. Help him to renounce his attitude of unforgiveness. Show him your amazing grace, mercy, love, and forgiveness, so he may forgive others. Humble his heart and spirit. In Jesus' name."

Batterers need to know that abuse is not an unpardonable sin. God wants to forgive them. They can find God's place of grace and mercy. A batterer needs to forgive himself. He will need to allow his wife and children to confront him with his past behaviors, in a safe environment, for the purpose of facing their fears. It will take time for his family to forgive and trust him again.

He will need to forgive the people in the past who abused him as a child. Why? Because this is the formula God has given to us for living in a fallen world. Do you want to get even, or get well? Forgiveness doesn't change the past, it takes the pain away from the memories. Forgiveness changes the present and the future. For big offenses done to us, it is not possible to forgive in our own human strength. We need God's power to help us.

Forgiveness means you give up the right to revenge. It means you trust God to judge, sentence, and punish your offenders. "...Never avenge yourself. Leave that to God, for he has said that He will repay those who deserve it." (Romans 12:19, LB)

We may not feel like forgiving our abusers, but as Christians, we walk by faith, not by feelings. We can make the effort and do our part;

God will do His part. Deal with forgiveness as a fact—not a feeling. If a person does not feel forgiven, he/she will have difficulty forgiving others. Emotions of unresolved guilt, bitterness, and resentment block the flow of feeling God's forgiveness and forgiving ourselves. To ask others to forgive us, we must agree with God that we have sinned.

Forgiving is not:
- minimizing the seriousness of the offense
- instant restoration of trust
- resuming the relationship without any changes

Forgiveness involves:
- genuine repentance
- restitution
- rebuilding trust

Helpers need spiritual discernment to know if the batterer is truly repentant or only pretending so as to get his family back. He needs to prove himself by his present and future behaviors. Forgiveness of past abuse is not easy or instant. It takes time. The test of forgiveness: when you can pray for your enemies, and when you can sincerely pray for the people who hurt you.

PROBLEM: Stress
TREATMENT: Stress management
TOOLS: Coping skills, prayer, relaxation, conflict resolution, communication, and problem solving skills
PRAYER: "Father, open my ears to listen and learn. Help me with my anxiety."
SCRIPTURES: 1 Peter 5:7, Luke 12:22-31
INTERCESSORY PRAYER: "Father, help ____ to relax and trust in you. Help him to learn skills to reduce his stress level. Encourage him to read the Bible for strength and comfort. In Jesus' name."

Stress triggers our emotions, then our emotions escalate. A negative coping skill must be replaced with a positive coping skill. Telling a batterer to stop without giving him tools to practice with is fruitless. Reading the Book of Proverbs is an excellent way to learn about ourselves.

Financial stress is often an issue. We tie our financial distress to our spiritual rest. We worry, and forget that God put the solution to money problems in His book: tithing, budgeting, working, and wisdom. A referral to a Christian financial counselor would be appropriate. I recommend books and programs by Larry Burkett, a well-known Christian author and financial planner.

Many batterers whose wives do not work outside the home perceive the income to be theirs alone. Financial pressures may exacerbate violence, but it does not cause it.

PROBLEM: Low to No Self-esteem
TREATMENT: God-esteem
TOOLS: God's view of His Children, rating scales, inventories
PRAYER: "Father, help me to see me as You see me. I ask for this by the blood of Christ."
SCRIPTURES: Titus 3:4-7, John 3:16, 2 Corinthians 12:9-10
INTERCESSORY PRAYER: "Father, give ____ an identity in Christ. Show him the great value he has to You. Help him to love himself as You love him, so that he may learn to love his wife and children the Godly way. In Jesus' name."

Batterers have a distorted view of themselves. They possess feelings of insecurity and powerlessness. These negative beliefs lead to excessive controlling behaviors. Batterers often exhibit narcissistic self-images, but this is a cover-up for feelings of inadequacy.

Belief in self is not the answer. This is the answer the world gives. Belief in God and God's view of us is the key to developing a healthy opinion of self. We are unworthy, but not worthless. Our definition of self-esteem is the value persons have because God created them in His image. Use a rating scale of 1-10 and ask the batterer to pick a number where he believes his self-esteem is operating. He may pick a zero, which shows he thinks he is worthless. Helpers are called to be encouragers and God-esteem boosters.

Self-esteem is a foundation from which self-respect, self-trust, and self-acceptance will manifest. You can only give to others what you possess. Love your neighbor as yourself implies that we need to first love ourselves (a godly love, not an egotistical, distorted love).

Men usually tie their self-esteem to their occupations. Help them to separate their value of who they are from what they do to earn a living. The gift of grace and salvation is free. God does not love pastors or missionaries more than He loves people in other professions. God loves who we are more than He loves what we do.

Your self-concept is composed of attitudes and beliefs you have about yourself. These beliefs determine what you think and what you do. Internal beliefs are powerful. Negative beliefs keep you stuck and stagnant. Teach batterers to challenge faulty beliefs and attitudes.

PROBLEM: Lack of Social Skills
TREATMENT: Learn and practice social skills.
TOOLS: Men's prayer group, accountability partner
PRAYER: "Father, help me to make godly men friends."
SCRIPTURES: 1 Corinthians 15:33, Proverbs 15:22
INTERCESSORY PRAYER: "Father, help ____ to trust his brothers and sisters in Christ. Help him to stay accountable to his pastor. In Jesus' name."

Batterers isolate the family from intimate contact with others in order to keep the secret of domestic violence. They are jealous of other relationships. They are often loners with no close male friends, but they may have many drinking buddies or fishing pals.

Many batterers did not learn the social skills needed to function in society, while others are experts at social manipulation. They mistrust people and think the world is out to get them. This is an excuse to blame others.

A few batterers can project the exact opposite behavior. They are charming—to other women. People like to be around them. They are fun at parties as long as they are the center of attention.

PROBLEM: Mental Illness: Depression, Post Traumatic Stress Disorder (P.T.S.D.), etc.
TREATMENT: Christian psychiatrist/medication
TOOLS: Long-term counseling with a Christian licensed professional counselor/Christian psychologist/Christian psychiatrist
SCRIPTURES: 2 Corinthians 1:8-9, Matthew 12:20, James 5:13-16
INTERCESSORY PRAYER: "Father, heal the emotions of ____. Give him encouragement and understanding of his illness. Heal his mind, will, and emotions. Touch his soul and spirit. Reveal the cause of his affliction. In Jesus' name."

The area of our brain that houses our emotions can become sick and unbalanced just like any part of our physical body. Medications are a gift from God. People with physical diseases use medication (heart disease, cancer, high blood pressure, diabetes, etc.). People with emotional diseases may also need medication. Christians with clinical depression caused by a malfunction in the brain chemicals often refuse medication because of the stigma attached to emotional illnesses. Antidepressant medications are not addictive. A Christian psychiatrist can diagnose and treat clinical depression with medication and counseling. Other types of depression can be treated with counseling without medication. It is not a sin to have depression or to seek treatment.

Depression caused by demonic oppression needs to be addressed by experienced religious professionals gifted in deliverance ministries. Medical and mental illnesses need to be ruled out first, as many of these symptoms mimic demonic attacks.

People with emotional illnesses build layers of protection around their emotions. This is a defense system the human body uses to protect us from emotional pain; but these layers also block the flow of the positive emotions of love, joy, compassion, etc. In counseling, these layers are peeled away carefully so the batterer may heal.

When should a pastor/helper refer a batterer to a psychiatrist, psychologist, or professional mental health counselor? When the batterer's problem(s) are beyond the helper's area of expertise. For example:
- Severe mental illness: hallucinations or delusions
- History of suicide attempts/homicide attempts
- Habitual substance abuse
- Childhood sexual abuse
- Post Traumatic Stress Disorder (P.T.S.D.)
- Severe head trauma
- Personality Disorders: Narcissistic, Antisocial, etc.

Pastors are experts in spiritual counseling, theology, and doctrine. Christian mental health counselors are experts in treating the subconscious and conscious brain, memories, and physical causes. The whole person needs to receive treatment and healing. Christian helpers can work together to provide total healing. If the client signs a release form, the mental health counselor can communicate with the pastor.

Studies show that men in the military often abuse their wives. Vietnam Veterans and Desert Storm Veterans need to be assessed for P.T.S.D. by a psychiatrist.

PROBLEM: Guilt and Shame
TREATMENT: Explore negative and positive guilt; explore the shame game.

TOOLS: Confession of positive guilt and discarding of negative guilt
PRAYER: "Father, help me to know the difference. I ask for Holy Spirit conviction."
SCRIPTURES: Matthew 23:32 and 35
INTERCESSORY PRAYER: "Father, convict the heart of _____ so that he may repent and be in a right relationship with You again. Take away his false guilt and shame. There is no condemnation for those in Christ Jesus. In Jesus' name."

Positive guilt leads to repentance. We see the wrong, hurtful actions we have committed. The Holy Spirit convicts us to lead us back to Jesus. Negative guilt leads to condemnation. The Bible states: "There is therefore now no condemnation for those who are in Christ Jesus". (Romans 8:1)

Many battering men have been taught a shame-based spirituality: having problems is sinful, and emotions are sinful. The fall damaged our mind, soul, and body; therefore, problems are a part of our humanness. But Christ teaches us the responsibility of dealing with our problems.

PROBLEM: Fear of Abandonment and Rejection
TREATMENT: Security in Christ and acceptance
TOOLS: Process past memories of childhood abandonment and face fears
PRAYER: "Father, help me to feel secure in Your love. I know You accept me for being me. I am totally accepted by God. I am God's purchased possession by the plan of redemption."
SCRIPTURES: Psalm 27:10, Mark 15:43, Psalm 10:14
INTERCESSORY PRAYER: "Father, You have not given _____ the spirit of fear, but of power and love and of a sound mind. Help him to feel secure in Your love. In Jesus' name."

Battering men who grew up in homes without fathers carry around a fear of being abandoned again by their loved ones. They are insecure and do not know why, or they believe it was because they were bad. Childhood rejection breeds adult insecurity and fear. Fear grows if you feed it. Batterers feed their fears with suspicion, lies, and anxiety.

If he continues to batter, his greatest fear will become a reality—his wife and children will leave him. He will cause the one thing he fears the most by his violent behavior. He will hold on so tightly, he will emotionally suffocate and alienate his family. Fear breeds more fear. Fear of failure produces anxiety and stress. Batterers fear change. Change is unknown territory.

Helpers can accept the batterer for who he is while rejecting the violent behaviors. Helping him to separate the person from the behavior will increase his feelings of security. He can understand how his wife, who loves him, still chooses to temporarily leave him until safety and restoration are completed. God loves the sinner, but rejects the sin. The person needs to learn that God will never leave him. For my father and mother have forsaken me, but the Lord will take me up. (Psalm 27:10)

PROBLEM: Unsubmissive to the Authority of God
TREATMENT: Correct biblical view of submission to God
TOOLS: Trust, security in God's unconditional love
PRAYER: "Father, help me to trust in Your promise to love me no matter what I do. Help me to submit to Your authority."
SCRIPTURES: Ephesians 5:21, Psalms 81:15, 1 Peter 5:5, Hebrews 12:9, James 4:7, 1 Peter 2:13
INTERCESSORY PRAYER: "Father, show _____ the purpose of submission and that it brings us closer to You. Help him to be under Your authority. In Jesus' name."

Batterers are in rebellion to the authority of God. They view submission as weakness. Submission requires a trusting heart. Batterers do not trust God and therefore fear submission. Would you submit and put your life into the hands of someone you didn't trust? Would you jump out of an airplane without a parachute? Trust is foundational, and must take place before submission to God can be achieved.

God is one hundred percent good. If humans could get this one point straight, they would not blame God when something bad happens. Instead, they would examine their own lives to find the problem.

PROBLEM: Unhealthy Boundaries
TREATMENT: Learn healthy boundaries.
TOOLS: Consequences of violating another person's physical boundary
PRAYER: "Father, help me to view my wife as a gift and not as a possession or my own personal property."
SCRIPTURES: Acts 20:35, Romans 12:10

INTERCESSORY PRAYER: "Father, help ____to cherish his wife and children and to respect their physical bodies. Help him to understand healthy boundaries and to not violate his wife and children. In Jesus' name."

When you purchase a home, a surveyor will mark the boundary lines to your property. No other person can violate your piece of earth. It is under your legal ownership. A person's physical body deserves the same respect. The boundary lines of batterers were often violated during childhood. As adults, they view their wives and children as personal property. They become enraged when someone tries to intervene to help their families. He sees his perceived ownership being questioned; imagine how you would react if your neighbor came to your house and loaded up your kitchen appliances. Batterers possess a distorted view of personal boundaries. They feel justified in this distorted thinking and react with violence when their families try to seek safety. Christians are purchased by the blood of Jesus Christ, and we are His legal property. Batterers trample the cross when they abuse God's families.

PROBLEMS: Selfishness and Sinful Pride
TREATMENT: Humility and repentance
TOOLS: Scripture, confession, awareness, practice of positive behaviors, and the power of our choices
PRAYER: "Father, humble me and take away my sinful pride. Redeem and cleanse me. I confess and renounce my sinful pride in the name of Jesus."
SCRIPTURES: Philippians 3:7 and 3:18-19, Job 35:12, Proverbs 11:2 and 16:18
INTERCESSORY PRAYER: "Father, help ____give up his foolish pride and selfishness. Humble him and show him how you gave up your life for him on the cross. In Jesus' name."

Do nothing from selfishness or empty conceit, but with humility of mind let each of you regard one another as more important than himself... (Philippians 2:3) The batterer's motto is, "I want what I want, and I want it now." He is like a child who wants all the toys in the sandbox.

Pride is a conceited sense of superiority.[2] The origin of pride is Satan. (Isaiah 14:13-15) Pride is evil and defiles men. (Mark 7:22-23) Pride and selfishness give Satan a foothold and harden the heart and mind, which produces spiritual decay. Satan was thrown out of heaven due to pride, rebellion and disobedience. (Isaiah 14:12-15) Satan craved sinful power and elevated "self". The result was a holy angel turned into a violent demon. Domestic violence in Christian homes has the mark of Satan's handiwork. 2 Corinthians 11:3 states that Satan deceived Eve by appealing to her pride (elevation of self to be equal with God). He uses the same trick to deceive the batterer. Satan serves the trinity of me, myself, and I.

Living for self is directly opposed to living for Jesus Christ. Selfishness is a root cause of conflict and strife. James declared, "Where envy and self-seeking exit, confusion and every evil thing will be there." (James 3:16) Can love and selfishness co-exist in a marriage filled with domestic violence? Selfishness demands a "me-first" philosophy and spawns self-righteousness. Violence is one of the rotten fruits of selfishness and pride.

An Exercise for the Batterer:
- Make a list of your own faults.
- Ask a Christian friend, accountability partner or pastor to list your faults.
- Examine your motives with a magnifying glass.
- Use the Bible as your standard when judging right and wrong.
- List the ways you are like Jesus.
- Ask God to reveal your selfishness.
- Evaluate your attitudes.
- Surrender your selfishness to God.
- Pray for the Holy Spirit to convert you instantly when you are selfish.
- Identify selfish thoughts, motives, and behaviors.

Practice UNSELFISH Behaviors:
- Wash dishes, do laundry, and help clean the house.
- Baby-sit the children and give your wife a rest.
- Take the family out to dinner and ask them to choose the restaurant.
- Pick up the dry-cleaning.
- Give the television remote control to your wife.
- Go to the grocery store for your wife.
- Play games with the children.
- Ask your wife to make a handyman list of projects to complete.

PROBLEM: Sense of Meaninglessness and Despair
TREATMENT: Find God's purpose for your life.
TOOLS: *12 Steps to Christian Recovery* (see chapter six), Book of Ecclesiastes
PRAYER: "Father, help me to love and serve You. Show me how, where, when, and what."
SCRIPTURES: Matthew 22:37, Mark 1:17, Mark 12:30-31
INTERCESSORY PRAYER: "Father, help ____ to abide in Christ. Give him the desire to seek Your face. Show him the purpose of loving and serving You. In Jesus' name."

Solomon went through a desert experience in his life, when despair filled his days. Apathy is a symptom of depression. Feelings of meaninglessness convey a lack of spiritual hunger for the things of God—a spiritual depression. Batterers become like Solomon, shouting, "Vanity of vanities! All is vanity!" They are pessimistic, paranoid, and ambivalent. Solomon's conclusion: "Fear God and keep His commandments, because this applies to every person. For God will bring every act to judgment, everything which is hidden, whether it is good or evil." (Ecclesiastes 12:13-14)

Adam's job was to take care of the Garden of Eden. Eve was his helper in the garden. We were created to have meaningful occupations while on this earth. God has given each person a special talent for employment. Jesus was a carpenter for thirty years before he started his three-year ministry and went to the cross as our Savior. Peter was a tent-maker, teacher, and evangelist. Sending the person in recovery to career counseling will be helpful. Christian career counselors or pastors can help the person discover his spiritual gifts.

After counseling and restoration of the family is completed, helpers can recommend the men to volunteer to help other male abusers. Service to others will give them a sense of purpose in God's kingdom. Recovered men are desperately needed to be role models for male teenagers and adults involved in domestic violence situations.

Each batterer should be assigned the reading of *Man's Search for Meaning* by Viktor Frankl. Frankl wrote his book after being released from a Nazi concentration camp during the Jewish holocaust. Hopefully the batterer will see in himself the abuse of power and the controlling behaviors of the German guards. The innocent prisoners suffered all types of abuse at the hands of their caretakers. The meaning of life is woven throughout the pages of this book. Frankl discovered that helping your fellow man is the utmost purpose of daily living.

Domestic Violence/Demoniac Violence

Satan is the ultimate source of violence and evil in the lives of believers, unbelievers, the church, society, and the world. Christians cannot ignore the part Satan and his demons play in domestic violence.

Dr. Ed Murphy, in his book, *The Handbook for Spiritual Warfare*, remarks:

> "Second to Satan's hatred of God is his hatred for humanity made in the image of God. Every blow against the welfare of humanity is a blow against God and His Kingdom. Women and children are the most vulnerable, so the evil one stimulates violence against women and abuse of children. Satan seems to hate women intensely. (Gen. 3:1ff). Little wonder! Only women give birth to children, and women traditionally have given stability to our homes. By corrupting or destroying women, Satan defeats God's purpose for humanity. Yet, children are even more vulnerable, and over the long term, injuring children damages humanity more than attacking adults. If Satan can cause children unspeakable pain through the adults they unhesitatingly trust, then Satan has accomplished the ultimate evil."[3]

How do Christians address domestic/demoniac violence?
- Prayer: intercession, warfare praying, fasting and prayer
- Deliverance ministries for Christians experiencing demoniac oppression
- Reading and using the Bible to fight Satan and his demons
- Identify violent behaviors as sin which must be confessed

Wesley L. Duewel in his book, *Mighty Prevailing Prayer*, states:
> "There are physical, financial, and spiritual needs that call for prevailing prayer. Homes are being torn apart by Satan, lives are being destroyed, and churches need God's special answers. We must prevail for ministries of the church and Christian organizations. We must prevail for moral and spiritual needs of our nation...Today, by mighty prevailing prayer, by using the authority Jesus has given us—the authority of His name, His cross, and His resurrection—we can restrain Satan's activities in many significant ways. We can bind and restrain his demon cohorts, back them off from

places they claim for Satan, and help the Spirit set Satan's captives free...The blood of Jesus, so precious to us, is a terrifying weapon against Satan...Satan cannot stand before the blood. Satan cannot fight the blood of Jesus and must flee from its reminder. It is your battle cry; it is your spiritual weapon. Use it to defeat Satan. Plead and praise the blood of Jesus, and drive Satan from the battlefield."[4]

Church Discipline and Batterers

The body of Christ (the church) must intervene when a member of the congregation is found to be guilty of abusing his/her family. The church (pastors, elders, deacons, leaders) must hold batterers accountable to ensure safety for the wives and children. Church leaders who abuse their families must also be held accountable when charged with domestic violence. The Bible gives the characteristics of a person in church leadership, and domestic violence is a disqualifier. (1 Timothy 3:2-3 and Titus 1:7)

Francis Frangipane in his book, *The Three Battlegrounds*, states: "There are God-ordained procedures to initiate corrections within a church. These corrections should be done by 'you who are spiritual...in a spirit of gentleness;...looking to yourself, lest you too be tempted.' Your motive should be to 'restore such a one.'" (Galatians 6:1) [5]

True Story

Kate and Doug attended one counseling session. A middle-aged pastor and his wife. Doug was the pastor for a large affluent church. Both were impeccably dressed and very attractive. Kate cried as she softly spilled their story. For twenty years, she endured Doug's constant criticism, temper, and controlling behaviors. Every night at 5 PM when Doug's car pulled into the driveway, her stomach would churn. The children would have to be quiet; seen and not heard. Kate played referee all during their teen years. Doug was a strict taskmaster without mercy. Was the house clean enough? Was Kate being a good pastor's wife? For twenty years she walked on eggshells. Kate reached the breaking point. Her bags were packed for a temporary separation. Doug showed up for marital counseling. He was desperate. Kate was serious; not once in twenty years had she threatened to leave him.

Doug agreed to do anything to save the marriage—anything but change. A few minutes alone with Doug revealed he was a perfectionist who believed his family and congregation needed a strong, flawless leader. He would never show weakness or vulnerability. This couple did not return for marital counseling.

Chapter Six

Batterer to Believer

Christian Support/Treatment/Education Groups for Male Batterers

What is the value of a men's group?

Support groups are scriptural:
- where two or more are gathered in His name (Matthew 18:20)
- confess your faults to one another (James 5:16)
- pray earnestly for one another (James 5:16)
- bear one another's burdens (Galatians 6:2)

Bootstrap therapy is not part of God's plan—pulling yourself up by your bootstraps by yourself. Christians need other Christians. Lone Rangers will not survive.

The support group is a rehearsal for marital and family counseling. The recovering batterers can bounce new ideas off each other and practice learned anger management skills, before trying the skills with wives and children. There is also the opportunity for:
- accountability partners
- practicing new behaviors
- validation of feelings by other men
- correction of wrong thinking
- correction of faulty belief systems
- acceptance by other men
- confrontation by other batterers
- encouragement to change by others
- forgiveness issues
- understanding by other batterers
- emotional safety to reveal childhood abuse
- enjoy fellowship with believers
- read the Bible and pray for each other

One goal of the Christian support group is to return the person back to his church, restored and healed. God does provide solutions to our problems.

Jesus surrounded himself with twelve men. Perhaps this group was the first Christian support group. These were men with many things in common; yet there was one central figure in this group, and His name was Jesus. Jesus held the group together. There was something magnetic that drew the twelve to Him. The disciples knew He was the source of life. Even before the thoughts took shape in their minds and the words formed on their lips, they knew in their spirits that Jesus was no ordinary man. And soon the twelve knew the truth—He was the son of God, the Messiah, the Savior, wonderful Counselor, mighty God, eternal Father, and Prince of Peace.

Jesus is the central figure in a Christian support group. He is the source of living water and of the bread of life. He is the ONLY way, the ONLY truth, and the ONLY light.

Support/Treatment/Education Groups for Christian Males Who Batter

The primary goals of groups must be:
1. to prioritize safety for women and children
2. to end violent, controlling, and abusive behaviors of abusers
3. to hold men accountable for the violence and abuse
4. to address their personal relationship with Jesus Christ
5. to challenge their faulty belief system about negative views of women in religious communities and in society and to promote an equal balance of marital power
6. to change negative thinking, attitudes, and behaviors

The secondary goals of groups must be:
1. to end emotional, verbal, sexual, economic, spiritual, and parental authority abuse
2. to prepare for future marital and family counseling

Treatment consists of:

confession	stress management
repentance	relaxation techniques
expectations of women explored	deliverance
correct biblical view of submission	communication skills
renewing of mind by the scriptures	peer confrontation
root causes of violence	making restitution
accountability and confrontation	Bible reading and prayer
problem solving and conflict resolution	asking forgiveness
anger management	balance of marital power
non-violent parenting skills	

The batterer needs assessment for the following:
- lethality: suicidal or homicidal
- low reading level or learning disabilities
- severity of injuries to children and any reports to Children's Services
- mental illnesses: depression, post traumatic stress disorder, personality disorders
- severity of injury to wife/partner
- physical/medical problems
- use of weapons
- past head trauma
- prior criminal records
- alcohol and drug abuse/other addictions
- court-ordered counseling
- past sexual childhood abuse

Duration of Groups:
Twenty-four weeks (six months), at a minimum of two hours per session.

Breaking Through the Denial System of Batterers

False beliefs:
- I only pushed her a little and she fell and hurt herself.
- She is not really hurt. She just wants attention.
- She pushed my buttons and made me angry.
- It is a woman's job to meet all my needs.
- I have to keep her in line.
- She makes me lose control of my temper.
- The alcohol makes me crazy and then I hit her.

Most batterers do not believe they are batterers. They believe it is a woman's place to meet their every physical, emotional, and sexual request. When she fails to perform her duties correctly, he believes it is his inalienable right to discipline her. If she is hurt by the physical battering, he minimizes the incident. Most batterers are pathologically jealous and feel justified when they abuse their wives, because supposedly "she was flirting with the cashier or the waiter or the mailman, etc." He believes he is justified in protecting his property rights by violence.

Many batterers see themselves as the victims when they are arrested for domestic violence. They blame the wives, police officers, and the legal system. Many batterers blame the modern feminists for turning society against men, and claim that all these liberated women must be lesbians. One abuser accused his wife of verbally and emotionally abusing him by not meeting all his needs and that's why he had to assault her.

Leaders of male support group for batterers report the consistency of the denial and blame systems of participants. This process of rationalization is universal to batterers.

It is imperative for helpers, pastors, and counselors to address the batterer's denial system with confrontation and truth. Tell them there is no excuse for domestic violence. This theme must be repeated until the truth is accepted. Batterers need to hear the message from other Christian men. Pastors and Christian men and women can unite to form a powerful team to convey the message: THERE IS NO EXCUSE FOR DOMESTIC VIOLENCE.

12 STEP Christian Recovery Program for the Batterer

1. Give God control of my life and admit I am NOT powerless over my violent behaviors.
2. Confess that I have sinned by abusing my wife and children. Allow wife and children to confront me in a safe environment to help with their healing process.
3. Ask forgiveness from God and from my family. Make restitution to my family.
4. Commit to daily prayer, Bible reading, and regular church attendance.
5. Attend a Christian support/treatment group for male batterers.
6. Attend pastoral or Christian counseling until recovery is complete.
7. Be accountable to my pastor or a trusted friend for my behaviors.
8. Be a Holy Spirit responder and tune in to the Holy Spirit who resides in me. Plug into God as the source of my strength and not rely on my own strength. Seek healing from the Great Physician, God.
9. Ask for help from trustworthy Christians when I need it.
10. Accept that I have choices in every situation: choice of attitude and choice of behavior.
11. Realize that my primary purpose on earth is to love, glorify, and serve God. Realize that my secondary purpose is to love my neigh-

bor as myself (the godly way) and that I first need to love myself before I can really love my family.
12. Help others recover from being batterers and teach them what I have learned.

Affirmation Statements:
1. God will forgive me if I ask.
2. I can change with the help of the Holy Spirit.
3. I can unlearn violent behaviors.
4. I will heal with the help of Jesus.
5. I have great value to Jesus.
6. My family can be restored.

Daily Formula for Living
A. When I feel like battering today I will:
 1. immediately leave the area to be alone.
 2. express what I am feeling to God and ask the Holy Spirit to calm me down.
 3. express what I am feeling to myself.
 4. express what I am feeling to a trustworthy person.
 5. identify the emotion and try to discern what I need at that moment.
 6. ask for help from my accountability partner.
 7. practice the anger management skills I learned.
 8. analyze the situation after I am calm.
 9. pat myself on the back for my recovery process.

B. Every morning I will:
 1. Commit the day to God before I get out of bed.
 2. Pray and read the Bible. Read one Psalm every morning.
 3. Be aware that I have choices in every situation.
 4. Be good to myself by thinking positive thoughts about myself.
 5. Practice anger management skills.

C. Every night I will:
 1. Read one proverb. Pray for my family and myself.
 2. Sleep the number of hours I need for my body.
 3. Practice anger management techniques.

D. Every week I will:
 1. Attend my support group meetings and/or Christian AA/NA meetings if necessary.

2. Attend church services.
3. Exercise with a physical activity.
4. Get myself permission to have fun by doing an activity I enjoy.

Pastors can help the person to create his own daily formula. The formula can be changed as the person changes and recovers. The batterer needs to be accountable to the pastor or counselor for following through with his formula.

Words About Healing:
John and Paula Sanford, in *The Transformation of the Inner Man*, state:

> "Psychologists would mend our self-images so that we could have confidence *in our selves*. Christ would slay all our fleshly self-confidence so that our only self-image becomes, I can do all things *through Him* who strengthens me.(Phil.4:13) A self-image is something *we* build, in which we falsely learn to trust. The world would fix the broken thing and rebuild personal pride and confidence. The Lord says, We'll fix it by not mending it at all! We'll use that broken thing to give glory to God, and from that awareness of sin we will build a trust every day anew in God's Holy Spirit to sing the beauty of Christ's nature through us for all to see."[1]

Fred Littauer in *The Promise of Restoration* states:

> "I have never been more convinced than I am today that only by God's unique ability and supernatural power can any of us be healed of the adult manifestations of childhood trauma and dysfunction. Many hurting people spend years and countless dollars seeking help and healing from counselors, psychologist and psychiatrists, only to realize that they haven't been healed. They have been helped, but the ability to heal emotional wounds has never been given to man, any more than the ability to heal physical wounds has ever been given to a doctor. A doctor can help. He can lance the would, he can cleanse it, he can treat it, but it has not been given unto him to heal it."[2]

Spiritual Inventory for the Batterer

1. Does Jesus control all areas of my life? (Luke 14:33)
2. Do I hate sin? (Psalm 119:104)
3. Is my thought life pleasing to God? (Philippians 4:8 and 9)
4. Do I have roots of bitterness? (Hebrews 12:15)
5. Do I have a clear conscience? (Acts 24:16)
6. Do I have a forgiving heart? (Matthew 6:15)
7. Is there fruit in my life to show my growth? (John 15:16)
8. Am I accountable to a mature Godly man? (James 5:16)
9. Am I nurturing my marriage? (Ephesians 5:29)
10. Am I honoring my wife? (1 Peter 3:7)
11. Am I examining myself honestly? (1 Corinthians 11:28)
12. Are the 3 B's consistent in my life: Bible, Beliefs, and Behaviors?
13. Am I practicing and living by the Ten Commandments?
14. Am I practicing the ABC Method?

Accept my problems. I admit I am a batterer.
Believe God will help me. Believe my family will be restored.
Change my thoughts and behaviors with help from my pastor and support group.

"Heavenly Father, I pray for the healing of these men. I plead the blood of Jesus for their lives and safety. Send Christian men to minister to their needs. I pray for renewed minds, hearts, souls, and spirits. Give them your peace. I pray these things in Jesus' name. Amen."

Activity on Anger for Recovering Batters

DIRECTIONS: Look up each scripture reference and write it. Meditate daily on these verses. Ask the Holy Spirit to help you.

1. Ephesians 4:26 & 27

_____
_____
_____

2. **Ephesians 4:31**

3. **Galatians 5:20**

4. **Colossians 3:8 & 10**

5. **James 1:19 & 20**

6. **Psalms 4:4**

7. **Ecclesiastes 7:7-9**

8. **Romans 7:21**

9. **Romans 12:19 & 21**

10. **Romans 14:13**

11. **1 Peter 2:1**

12. Proverbs 7:9

13. Proverbs 14:29

14. Proverbs 16:32

15. Proverbs 19:11

16. Proverbs 29:11

17. Proverbs 29:22

What does God say about anger?

How can the Holy Spirit help you to control your violent behavior?

What is anger?

How can you take responsibility for your own anger?

_____
_____
_____

How do you create your own feelings of anger, which lead to rage and destruction?

_____
_____
_____
_____

ABC's of Jesus Therapy for Christian Men

Admit: Admit you assaulted/abused your wife to control her.

Believe: Believe and have faith that God will heal you and restore your family.

Confess: Confess the **sin** of domestic violence, repent, and make restitution to those you hurt.

Deliverance: Deliverance from Satan's strongholds, demonic violence, and generational domestic violence. Cover yourself with the blood of Jesus.

Emotions: Emotional healing is needed for past childhood abuse.

Forgiveness: Ask God to forgive you. Forgiveness of self, forgive past abusers, ask wife and children to forgive you.

Glorify: Glorify God for His saving grace, mercy and the cross of Jesus.

Holy Spirit: Ask the Holy Spirit who dwells in you to change you on the inside and outside.

Importance: It is important that you attend a Christian support group for male batterers.

Jehovah Rapha: Call upon Him to transform your mind, soul, spirit, and body.

Knowledge: Gain knowledge and education about anger management and practice these skills. Learn your triggers and physical body cues.

Love:	Love your wife as Jesus loves the church and practice mutual submission. Jesus did not abuse His church.
Mend:	Mend your relationships by being honest, accountable and trustworthy.
Never:	Never assault your wife again. The consequences are the loss of your family and prison.
Obedience:	Be obedient to the authority of God, the laws of society, and your church.
Pray:	Pray daily for yourself, wife, and family.
Quiet:	Spend quiet time with the Lord each day for strength.
Read:	Read your Bible daily to renew your mind through the scriptures. "Memory healing" can be accomplished by His word, Holy Spirit, and a trained counselor.
Stop:	Stop making excuses, blaming others, and believing Satan's lies.
Transformation:	The old nature will pass away. Seek this with all your heart.
Understand:	Understand the root causes of domestic violence.
Victory:	You can have victory over your addictions to power and control.
Worship:	Worship God weekly at your place of worship or church.
X-ray:	X-ray your motives and the condition of your heart.
You:	You are solely responsible for your anger and violent behaviors.
Zero:	Zero in on your strengths and positive qualities.

True Story

Margaret, a committed Christian, knew Kyle drank alcohol when he visited the bar with his buddies after work. She married him anyway. She thought he would quit drinking and stay home after the wedding. Margaret was wrong.

Kyle did take the family to church on Sundays. The three girls adored their new stepfather. Kyle was kind, gentle, and soft-spoken when he was sober or drunk. He was a hard worker and provided well for his family.

After a few months of weekend binge drinking with his buddies, Margaret starting locking Kyle out of the house. Kyle would kick doors and break windows, but he never hit Margaret or the girls. After police intervention and threats of separation, Kyle attended Christian counseling with Margaret as well as a support group for Christian alcoholic male abusers. Kyle's biological father was an alcoholic and a batterer. He would often get Kyle out of bed late at night and force him to drink liquor with him. Kyle's stepfather was the opposite; a gentle and kind man. Kyle stayed sober for months at a time and would then binge drink. After a year, Kyle found Jesus, stopped drinking permanently, and legally adopted his three stepdaughters.

Chapter 7

Victim to Victor

10 Days of Devotions from the Psalms

Day 1, Psalm 31:20

Thou dost hide them in in a secret place from the conspiracies of man; Thou dost keep them secretly in a shelter from the strife of tongues.

God wants to shelter you for safety and protection God uses earthly instruments and dwellings to bring forth His plan of safety. There is a way out of the wilderness. Take the path that is offered. You will find hope and comfort.

"Father, we pray for angels of protection to surround the women who read these words."

Day 2, Psalm 30:5b

Weeping may last for the night, but a shout of joy comes in the morning.

Your tears break the heart of your Heavenly Father. Take heart for He sees your your tears and hears your cries. Joy will be restored to you, dear sister. You can find encouragement from other women who have healed from violence in their Christian homes.

"Father, comfort your daughters and draw near to them. Dry their tears."

Day 3, Psalm 44:21

Would not God find this out? For He knows the secrets of the heart.

Day 4, Psalm 94:19

When my anxious thoughts multiply within me, Thy consolations delight my soul.

You are so tired of pretending and keeping the secret. God knows your heart. He longs for you to choose to reveal the abuse in your home. Be wise. Ask for help. We will help you. Call us or call a domestic violence shelter in your area. Go to your pastor, friend, or family member. Seek safety and tell the secret.

"Father, show these women the way. Help them to speak the truth. The truth will set them free."

May the word of God sustain you as you try to survive in a violent home. But, be careful, lest your husband rob you of your joy in the Lord.

"Father, may your written word bring hope to her depressed soul and spirit. Saturate her in your love. Show her compassion."

Day 5, Psalm 91:1

He who dwells in the shelter of the most High will abide in the shadow of the Almighty.

God has provided domestic violence shelters for your safety. He will not force you to seek shelter. He will only offer it to you.

"Father, we pray she will seek shelter and safety.
We bind the violence
in her husband in the name of Jesus Christ."

Day 6, Psalm 72:12-14

He will rescue their life from oppression and violence; and their blood will be precious in His sight.

God wants to set you free from the prison of abuse. There can be victory for you. Spilled blood at the hands of your husband brings sorrow to the Lord.

"Father, we ask for the precious blood of Jesus to cover and protect her.
There is power in your blood. Set this captive free."

Day 7, Psalm 7:1

O Lord my God, in Thee I have taken refuge; save me from all those who pursue me and deliver me.

God will deliver you from death. Choose life. Choose to run to safety. You will find peace.

"Father, deliver this wife from death. We intercede with prevailing prayers for her very life."

Day 8, Psalm 118:5

From my distress I called upon the Lord; the Lord answered me and set me in a large place.

The Lord will set you in a place of peacefulness. Take courage and trust in Jesus. Ask for wisdom and discernment.

"Father, we call upon you to give her wisdom and spiritual discernment to make the right decisions."

Day 9, Psalm 146:7

Who executives justice for the oppressed; who gives food to the hungry. The Lord sets the prisoners free.

You are a prisoner in your home in a country of freedom. He tries to control your mind, heart, soul, spirit, and body. Jesus died to set you free.

"Father, release her mind, heart, soul, spirit, and body from his control, bondage, and the power of darkness. Give her strength through your Holy Spirit."

Day 10, Psalm 18:48

He delivers me from my enemies; surely Thou dost lift me above those who rise up against me; Thou dost rescue me from the violent man.

A battering husband is the enemy of God and shames your marriage which was created by God. God is full of mercy but also of justice. Violent men will stand before God and give an account of their abusive behaviors.

"Father, render justice and deliver this woman from her violent husband. We ask for the power of your Holy Spirit to cover her, guide her, and help her. We bind Satan and his evil plans to destroy this family. In Jesus name."

To the Christian Women Who are being Battered:

- You must seek safety and protection first, and then tell the secret of the abuse. Tell your pastor, your friends, your family members. Find a Christian counselor immediately. Go to a Christian domestic violence shelter or a secular shelter if a Christian shelter is not available. A shelter will help you to look at all your options before you make any decisions. It is <u>not</u> a sin to leave and seek safety.
- Go out of town to a friend's house if you will be safe there, and call your pastor, friends, and family members and tell them the secret.
- There are many domestic violence shelters in different states and counties, if you need to leave the state temporarily for protection.
- You and your children must be safe before any counseling can begin. Trial periods while the husband lives at a different location can eventually take place, after he has attended therapy for batterers and received pastoral counseling. Restoration will take time.
- You will need police intervention. God can use the county jail and prison to change and heal a batterer. It is not betrayal to ask the police for help. It is using wisdom to save your life and the lives of your children.
- Remember, you are not to blame for your husband's violent behavior and abuse. There is no excuse for domestic violence. Looking at a batterer's past and childhood helps in understanding his violent behavior, but it does not excuse it. Batterers were also the victims at one time—they need help to recover. You need to help yourself first, but you will also help him by telling the secret and leaving, or having him leave, until restoration is accomplished. Jesus is in the business of healing marriages. If the batterer will not stop the violence and accept help, then you do have choices.
- Victims, you can be victors! You, too, will need counseling to look at your own issues. Many of the battered women I have counseled suffered from low self-esteem and a poor self-image before they met their husbands. Many of them witnessed violence and/or alcoholism in their homes during childhood. You will need to heal emotionally and spiritually.

> *"Heavenly Father, I pray that you would send angels of protection around these women and children. I plead the precious blood of Jesus for their lives and safety. Please give them comfort, peace of mind, hope, encouragement, and understanding. I pray that you would send Christians into their lives to give them love and support. I pray that you would provide healing and restoration. I pray these things in Jesus' name. Amen."*

QUESTIONNAIRE TO IDENTIFY POTENTIAL ABUSIVE RELATIONSHIPS BEFORE MARRIAGE

Answer the following questions.

Are you in an unhealthy relationship?
Is he someone who:

- ❏ Believes men should be in control and powerful and women should be passive and submissive?
- ❏ Expects you to serve him, obey him, and jump at his commands?
- ❏ Dictates what you can wear?
- ❏ Calls you several times a day at work?
- ❏ Accuses you of flirting with the pastor or with men at church?
- ❏ Expects you to be the perfect woman?
- ❏ Discourages you from making friends at church?

Are you in an abusive relationship?
Is he someone who:
- ❏ Has hit, pushed, or restrained you against your will?
- ❏ Has punched walls or broken your possessions?
- ❏ Blames you when he gets angry and loses his temper?
- ❏ Pressures you to have sex even though it's against your religion as a single person?
- ❏ Uses the Bible to tell you about your faults?
- ❏ Verbally degrades women in general?

If you are dating a man with the above behaviors, please seek godly counsel before you make the mistake of marrying him. He will not change after marriage. The abuse will escalate. If he will not agree to premarital counseling with a pastor or counselor, then it's your choice to end the relationship.

QUESTIONNAIRE
TO DETERMINE IF ARE YOU IN AN
ABUSIVE MARRIAGE

Is your husband someone who:
- ❏ Turned into a tyrant after the honeymoon?
- ❏ Falsely accuses you of adultery?
- ❏ Makes your family and friends concerned about your safety?
- ❏ Threatens you with harm to control you?
- ❏ Criticizes you for little things?
- ❏ Doesn't allow you to make any decisions in the home?
- ❏ Hits, pushes, or shakes you when he is angry?
- ❏ Misquotes scripture verses to force you into submission?
- ❏ Takes you to church on Sunday and physically beats you on Monday?
- ❏ Switches from lovingly sweet to explosively violent in a matter of minutes?
- ❏ Only gives you money for groceries and not for personal items?
- ❏ Follows you to work to check up on you?
- ❏ Calls you terrible names?
- ❏ Spends many evening away from home and says his whereabouts are none of your business?
- ❏ Makes you quit your job and stay home all day?
- ❏ Forces you to have sex whenever he wants sex?
- ❏ Breaks your bones or knocks out your teeth?

If you are in an abusive marriage, please seek help immediately. The abuse will continue to escalate. There is help available to you. Abusive behaviors follow a consistent pattern and are not isolated incidents.

Lies the Victims Tell Themselves About Domestic Violence
- It's my fault. I need to be a better wife.
- God is punishing me for my past sins.
- I need to just try harder to not make him angry.
- The Bible says I have to obey his every command no matter what.
- I can't tell anyone about his abusive behaviors and embarrass him.
- God loves everyone but me.
- Alcohol makes him violent. If he stops drinking, he won't hit me.
- When he gets a better job, he will stop the abuse.
- Good Christian wives submit to any sexual act their husbands want.
- He doesn't mean it when he calls me ugly names.
- I am fat and stupid like he says.
- If I pray more and read the Bible more, he will stop beating me.
- I can help him change by just loving him more and keeping quiet.
- If I cleaned the house better and had dinner on time every night, he wouldn't get so upset.
- I must be a bad person.
- I don't deserve nice treatment.
- I must be crazy and insane.
- I'm a terrible mother.
- No one will believe me if I tell them about his violent temper.
- The children don't know he hits me. I can keep it from them.
- I should dress like he says, so I won't entice other men.
- Only whores wear make-up, as he says.
- I should never disagree with anything he says. He is the head of the house.
- If I would learn to be more submissive, he would stop abusing me.

Myths About Domestic Violence in Christian Homes
Myth: Women like the abuse, or they would leave.
Truth: Women are afraid to leave, because the abusers threaten to kill them if they do.

Myth:	Women nag their husbands and make them explode in anger and hit them.
Truth:	Women may nag, but they still do not deserve to be assaulted. Men are responsible for their reactions.
Myth:	Women know how to push their husband's buttons to make them violent.
Truth:	We create our own anger, and no one can force us to hit anyone. Men choose to assault their wives.
Myth:	Some women tell their pastors they are being battered just to get attention.
Truth:	Christian women hide the secret of abuse for years, until they cannot tolerate it any longer.
Myth:	Christian men and pastors do not batter their wives. They are being targeted by male-bashing feminist groups.
Truth:	I have provided counseling to Christian couples and pastors' wives, and these men do abuse their wives.

Victims and healing

Jesus was beaten before he went to the cross. He did not deserve it. He was innocent. He was on a mission—to save the world from sin. He did not fight back. You are not on a mission to save the world from sin. You are not the Savior. You are not to be beaten by your husband/boyfriend. Jesus died to set you free—not to see you abused. It is a sin for a husband to beat his wife. There is a world of difference in dying for your belief in Christ and dying for no reason at the hands of your husband. We are called to lay down our lives for Jesus. We are not called to lay down our lives for an abusive husband. Jesus died to set the oppressed free. (Luke 4:18) Battered women are oppressed women.

Jesus was an innocent victim, as you are today. He was physically abused by the Romans. He was verbally and emotionally abused by the Jewish Pharisees and Sadducees, His own religious denomination. They criticized Him unmercifully. Jesus was abandoned by His twelve closest friends, the disciples. His friend and student, Judas, betrayed Him for the almighty dollar. Hanging a naked person on the cross for public viewing with only a small cloth to cover the private area is a form of sexual abuse. Jesus was a victim of violence. His family of faith turned against Him. Jesus knows exactly how you feel—turn to Him for comfort.

God, through His Holy Spirit, empowers powerless people. A "bleeding" spirit needs healing, just as a battered physical body needs healing.

Fear of death can be either a motivator to leave or a paralyzer. For women who experienced trauma in childhood, fear of death may increase depression and suicidal tendencies.

- Women, you need to know the risks so you can save your lives. Women who leave their batterers are at a seventy-five percent greater risk of being killed by the batterer than those who stay. (Barbara Hart, National Coalition Against Domestic Violence, 1988) The risk of death can be decreased by developing a crisis intervention plan.
- Domestic violence is the leading cause of injury to women between the ages of 15 and 44 in the United States—more than car accidents, muggings, and rapes combined. (Uniform Crime Reports, Federal Bureau of Investigation, 1991)

Are you afraid that people will not believe you are being abused? Jesus' own brothers at first did not believe He was the Messiah. Mark 3:21 states, "And when His own people heard of this, they went out to take custody of Him; for they were saying, 'He has lost His senses.' " If your own relatives or church friends do not believe you, take heart—Jesus knows the truth. Staff members at domestic violence shelters will believe you.

**He heals the brokenhearted and
binds up their wounds.
(Psalms 147:3)**

Victims and Codependency

Any female can become a victim of domestic violence. Quick courtships and short engagements do not allow women to know enough about their fiancées before marriage. The violent behaviors of their husbands are hidden until after the wedding ceremony. Christian women are potential targets because of their traditional views of submission and biblical family values. Christian batterers use this fact to take advantage of women. These batterers carry their Bibles to church and appear to be Godly men, but in reality they are dominating and controlling.

The issue of codependency among battered women is controversial. This section is not meant to label or blame the victims. She is NOT responsible for his violent behaviors. Not all victims of marital abuse suffer from codependency. Many women use survival behaviors to protect themselves and their children that to the outside counselor may look like codependent behaviors.

This issue must be addressed, because there are women who suffer from codependency, and they must be educated or they may marry another unhealthy mate. As a counselor, I have seen this cycle repeated. She divorces the abuser, only to marry another one. She is a product of generational domestic violence. Ezekiel 16:44 states, "As is the mother, so is her daughter." Women often marry a man who is just like their fathers. They are not aware of this cycle and the reasons they continue to choose abusive men. They do not want to be abused, and they do not like it. They possess low self-esteem and a poor self-image. Many of these women experienced violence in the dating relationship, but they married the abuser anyway.

Characteristics of Victims Who are Codependent:
- Low self-worth
- Weak personal boundaries
- Obsessed with care-taking of others; a fixer
- Fears abandonment and rejection
- Approval-seeking and a people pleaser
- Feels victimized
- Overdeveloped sense of responsibility for others
- Feels anxious or depressed
- Does not want to be alone

Abused Christian women accept the abuse as a way of life. The Hebrews were prisoners in Egypt and slaves to Pharaoh. They were beaten, degraded, and controlled. They had been in bondage for so long that abuse was accepted as a way of life. The Hebrews did cry out to God, and He gave them a way to escape. He sent Moses, and you know the rest of the story. God hears the cries of abused women today. He gives them a way of escape. He sends them to domestic violence shelters. He sends them resource guides written by survivors.

Helpers, pastors, and counselors need to teach Christian women the difference between being a servant and a doormat:

SERVANTS	**DOORMATS**
Healthy self-esteem	No self-esteem
Serve others out of love	Help others and neglect self
Filled with joy	Filled with guilt and shame
Healthy boundaries	No boundaries
Give unconditional love	Give extreme care-taking
Value self and others	Value others and not self

Fred Littauer, in *The Promise of Restoration*, states:
"Though they long for intimate relationships, adults raised in a stressful environment have great difficulty finding or establishing meaningful relationships. They have superficial relationships with others and often choose those who are having similar struggles. Abused women tend to be attracted to abusive men. An emotionally deprived person tends to bond with another person on a similar level of emotional pain. Victims tend to marry victims."[6]

Jan and Don Frank, in *When Victims Marry Victims*, state:
"If a woman has been a victim of abuse (physical, emotional, or sexual) in her childhood, she tends to marry someone from one of four types of backgrounds: first, one of abuse (physical, emotional, or sexual); second, an alcoholic or dry alcoholic; third, what I call a "rigid," often strictly religious home; or fourth, a home background where the person was emotionally deprived."[7]

Codependency Issues

TYPE A
- low self-esteem
- poor self-image
- experienced abuse in family of origin and exposed to domestic violence
- sexually abused as a child
- depression and mood swings
- witnessed abuse of mother by father or stepfather
- alcoholism in family tree
- finds salvation as a teenager

- will stay in the marriage and tolerate abuse in another mate if she becomes divorced. Victims marry victims.

TYPE B
- quiet and soft-spoken
- shy and sensitive
- easily intimated and passive
- raised in a devout, strict Christian home
- taught to be submissive to men at all costs
- conformist and follows rules
- caretaker of others
- wants to be a mother and homemaker
- easy-going personality
- exposed to verbal and emotional abuse but no physical abuse in childhood
- will stay in the marriage and hide the secret of domestic violence.

TYPE C
- not raised in a Christian home
- low self-esteem and poor self-image
- neglected as a child
- became pregnant before the marriage
- finds salvation after marriage, but her husband is unsaved and ridicules her faith
- husband still does drugs and alcohol
- will stay in a violent marriage and try to win her husband to Christ. She may object when he forbids her to attend church, pray, and read her Bible.

Women with codependency issues can be a mixture of the above characteristics. Again, I state that there is no excuse for domestic violence. Men choose to assault their wives/girlfriends.

Victim/Victor Language

Rudyard Kipling once stated, "Words are the most powerful drugs known." Words are the verbal result of what we think.

Victim Language

The words we use can project victim language and reveal that we see ourselves as victims.

<u>My internal dialogue</u>:
- I talk to myself.
- I listen to myself.
- I take action on my negative self-talk.
- If I choose to talk like a victim, I will listen like a victim, and I will act like a victim.

Victor Language

If I choose to talk like a victor, I will listen like a victor, and I will act like a victor.

Empower talk: "I have choices in every situation."
Empower listen: "I hear my choices."
Empower action: "I will act on my choices."

<u>My internal dialogue</u>:
- I talk to myself.
- I listen to myself.
- I take action on my positive self-talk.

I have power over what thoughts I want to think. I can question and disregard negative thoughts. I can choose what I say about myself.

Practice your internal dialogue:
_____
_____
_____
_____

Treatment for Victims

1. Christian support group for battered women
2. Individual counseling with a Christian counselor or pastor

Tools
1. Writing therapy:
   a) Write letters to batterer to release emotion (these letters are not to send)
   b) Write poetry
   c) Write your autobiography
   d) Use journaling or a diary
2. Genograph (see Tools Section)
3. Make a list of your strengths
4. Read books about domestic violence (see Resource Section)
5. Sign a no-suicide contract
6. Music therapy
   a) Listen to scriptures set to music
   b) Listen to tapes on relaxation or gospel music
7. Art therapy
   a) Draw or paint your feelings
   b) Use clay or chalk for expression
8. Permission therapy
   a) Permission to verbally express your anger for being battered by your mate
   b) Permission to use your anger to develop self-care
   c) Permission to cry, feel sad, and talk about the abuse
   d) Permission to accept help from others
   e) Permission to put safety before reconciliation

Medical Treatment
1. If your mate was unfaithful:
   a) AIDS/HIV test
   b) Test for sexually transmitted diseases: herpes, venereal warts, syphilis, gonorrhea, etc.
2. Physical exam for any internal/external physical problems caused by past battering
3. Assessment for anti-depressant medication by a medical doctor for clinical depression and treatment if necessary.

   I have talked with abused women who were misdiagnosed with bipolar disorder or schizophrenia and prescribed medication. Their problems were not due to mental illness. Their problems were caused by domestic violence. These women need to be re-evaluated by a Christian psychiatrist and the medication discarded if they are diagnosed to be without these disorders. I know wives whose husbands committed them to psychiatric hospitals. Their abusers wanted to "prove" their wives were "crazy." These wives continued to hide the secret of violence due to fear and the threats of the abusers: *"I'll put you in a state mental institution forever if you tell the doctors I beat you. It's your fault. You're the crazy one, not me. You'll never see your kids again."* These women are not mentally ill. They are suffering from domestic violence in their Christian homes.

<u>Issues to address</u>:
suicidal thoughts
homicidal thoughts
counseling for children
alcohol or drug abuse
depression or P.S.T.D.
anxiety and fear
guilt, shame and blame
denial
adult child of an alcoholic
anger and rage
childhood physical abuse

bitterness and resentment
forgiveness
setting boundaries
support system
spiritual condition
fear of abandonment and loneliness
past sexual child abuse
generational domestic violence
stress/distress
childhood emotional and verbal abuse
view of God as a father

Daily Formula for Living

A. When I feel like going back to my husband before it is safe, I will:
    1. Call a woman from my Christian support group
    2. Call my counselor or pastor
    3. Call a domestic violence shelter in my community
    4. Call a friend or family member
    5. Call a crisis hotline number
    6. Express and identify the emotion and question myself honestly:
        a) Am I feeling lonely?
        b) Am I feeling guilty?
        c) Is he pressuring me?
        d) Am I feeling sorry for him?
        e) Do I want sexual intimacy?
        f) Am I rushing the healing process?
        g) How will it affect the children?
        h) Do I want to take a chance on being battered again?
        i) Am I having financial difficulties?
    7. List all my options and choices. Tell myself I have options.

B. Every morning I will:
   1. Commit the day to God before I get out of bed
   2. Pray and read the Bible; read one Psalm per day
   3. Be aware that I have choices in every situation
   4. Be good to myself by thinking positive thoughts

C. Every night I will:
   1. Read one Proverb; pray for myself and my family
   2. Sleep the number of hours I need for my body
   3. Write in my journal about the events of the day

D. Every week I will:
   1. Attend my support group meetings
   2. Attend church services
   3. Exercise by doing a physical activity
   4. Give myself permission to have fun by doing an activity I enjoy

Counselors, pastors, and helpers can assist the person in creating her own daily formula. The formula can be changed as the person recovers.

Twelve-Step Christian Recovery Program For Victims
1. Admit there is a problem. Admit you need counseling and intervention.
2. Attend a Christian support group for female victims of domestic violence.
3. Commit to daily prayer, Bible reading, and regular church attendance.
4. Be accountable to a Christian friend or pastor.
5. Ask for help from trustworthy people when I need it.
6. Plug into the Holy Spirit as the source of my healing and not rely on my own strength.
7. Be a servant and not a doormat.
8. Confront my spouse in a safe environment with a counselor/pastor when appropriate.
9. Forgive my spouse. It will take time. Trust in God's timing for my healing and do not rush the process.
10. Attend marital and family counseling for restoration if the physical abuse has stopped and the abuser has attended a support/treatment/education group for male batterers.
11. Know that I have choices in every situation.

12. Realize that my primary purpose on earth is to love, glorify, and serve God. Realize that my secondary purpose is to love my neighbor as myself (the godly way), and that I first need to love myself before I can really love my family and others.

<u>Affirmation Statements:</u>
- I do not deserve to be abused. I do not like it or ask for it.
- I deserve to be safe in my own home.
- I am not the cause of his violent behaviors.
- I am not crazy, insane, or stupid.
- I have great value to Jesus.

Abigail, Nabal, and God

Abigail was married to Nabal during a time and in a culture where she had few external choices. Separating from her husband for a season was not a socially or culturally accepted option as it is today. Abigail nonetheless had internal choices, and she still chose to obey God. (1 Samuel 25:1)

Abigail's husband was a harsh man with an alcohol problem. He became wealthy by cheating his business associates. When King David asked Nabal to return a good deed, Nabal refused, due to his greed and selfishness. Nabal's servant immediately sought out Abigail for help, for King David threatened to kill the entire household and called his master "a worthless man." Abigail immediately coordinated the feeding of 600 hungry men. The servants obeyed her out of respect and without hesitation. The Bible tells us she was intelligent and beautiful. She alone saved the lives of the entire household.

God showed Nabal that He (God) was in control. Nabal was struck by God and died. (Verse 38) Abigail did not allow her unhappy marriage to an ungodly man to turn her into a woman of bitterness or resentment. She remained faithful to God by running her household fairly. God gave her a way to escape her abusive marriage. Abigail then became the wife of a king.

This story in the Old Testament shows the merciful and just characteristics of our God. He still rules the world, and He will not be mocked.

> ...I have set before you life and death, blessing and curses. Now choose life, so that you and your children may live and that you may love the Lord your God, listen to His voice, and hold fast to Him. For the Lord is your life...
> **(Deuteronomy 30:19-20)**

Chapter Eight

Trauma to Triumph

Twelve-Step Christian Recovery Program for Teenagers
1. Know I am not to blame for my parent's violent behavior.
2. Know I do not deserve to be abused in any way.
3. Believe I am an important human being.
4. Attend Christian counseling, family counseling, and youth group.
5. Talk about my problems with a trustworthy friend.
6. Express my feelings, even if I am feeling suicidal. Ask and accept help.
7. Pray and read Bible.
8. Stop self-destructive behaviors such as doing alcohol and drugs.
9. Confront my father/stepfather in a safe environment. Forgive parents/stepparents after they stop the violence and seek restoration.
10. Talk about anger instead of physically fighting others. Practice anger management.
11. Be a positive role model for younger sisters and brothers.
12. Accept myself.

<u>Affirmation Statements</u>:
- I am special to Jesus.
- I am loved by many people.
- I have value as a person.
- I can have a happy life.
- I will get through this.

Adolescence issues
   Adolescence is a period of life during which teenagers make the transition from childhood to adulthood. Adolescence is perhaps the most stressful time in a person's life—he/she is developing physically, emotionally, psychologically, spiritually, hormonally, socially, and sexually.
   Adolescents have great desires and needs:
- Need for self-acceptance and an identity
- Need for acceptance from their peers and the opposite sex

- Need for attention and recognition
- Need to explore the external world apart from the family

Adolescents have certain issues due to just being at this stage in life:
- Inferiority feelings
- Comparing body image to others
- Fluctuating self-esteem
- Hormonal mood swings
- Concern over sexual body changes

When the issue of domestic violence in the home is added, an adolescent can experience:

depression	teen pregnancy	truancy at school
suicidal tendencies	run away from home	anxiety
explosive anger	abuse siblings	eating disorders
no self-esteem	crime	self-mutilation
confusion	dating violence	nightmares
premarital sex	date rape	drop out of school
gang membership	change in peer group	drugs and alcohol
fluctuating grades	abuse mother/stepmother	

Both males and females may act out with negative behaviors:

MALES:
model father's violent behaviors
fighting at school
abuse siblings and pets
rebel against authority figures
join a gang
sell drugs

FEMALES:
premarital sex: attention seeking
codependency formation
teen pregnancy
tolerate abuse from boyfriend
mistrust of men
shoplifting

Crisis Intervention
1. suicide assessment
2. homicide assessment
3. runaway potential
4. alcohol/drugs
5. deviant behavior and crime
6. gang membership
7. abuse of siblings
8. physical and sexual abuse in home

Community Resources
1. Youth groups/youth pastors
2. Youth for Christ
3. Fellowship of Christian Athletes
4. Big Brothers/Big Sisters
5. High school counselors
6. Teen alcohol and drug programs
7. Community outreach programs
8. Mental Health Crisis Centers
9. Domestic Violence Coalitions
10. Counseling centers for adolescents
11. Tutors for school classes
12. Teen Hotlines
13. Campus Crusade for Christ

Treatment and areas to address:
1. Suicide intervention and prevention
2. Homicide intervention and prevention
3. Anger management skills
4. Conflict resolution
5. Problem solving skills and coping skills
6. Behavior management
7. Self-esteem issues
8. View of God as father
9. Relationship with father/stepfather
10. Relationship with mother/stepmother
11. Relationship with siblings
12. Christian AA and NA if applicable
13. Attitude
14. Anxiety and Stress
15. Mending the broken spirit
16. Abstinence issues/sex education
17. Generational domestic violence
18. Strengths
19. Depression
20. Sexual abuse
21. Physical abuse
22. Emotional abuse
23. Verbal abuse
24. Witnessing abuse to mother/stepmother
25. Witnessing abuse to siblings
26. Neglect of parents
27. Addictions: sex, pornography, etc.
28. Pregnancy, AIDS/HIV, and sexually-transmitted diseases

- Interviews with children living in battered women's shelters show that, within a one-year period, seventy-five percent of the children over fifteen years of age had run away twice.[1]
- Step families: Blended families experiencing domestic violence have an increased level of stress.
- Research shows that stepdaughters are six times more likely to be sexually abused than daughters who live with a natural family.[2]

- Sixty-three percent of boys aged eleven to twenty years who commit homicide, murder the man who was abusing their mother. (National Coalition Against Domestic Violence)

In violent homes, survival becomes a full-time job. In these homes, teens daily experience fear, denial, anger, inconsistency, chaos, and the potential threat of harm to their mothers, siblings, and self. Emotions become numb. They try to hide the secret from peers at church and school. They feel alone, angry, sad, confused, and hopeless. Emotions are suppressed for survival or, the opposite, they act out by modeling the behaviors of the batterer. They learn to live by a double standard—pretend we are a happy family at church, but at home it is very different. For many of these teenagers, the streets are safer than their own homes.

Coping skills for survival:
- lying to avoid being assaulted
- lying to batterer on behalf of mother to help her avoid an assault
- staying away from home as much as possible
- repressing or suppressing emotions

Helping our daughters:
If the cycle of violence is not stopped, daughters will grow up to tolerate abuse from a mate. They will search for love and accept sex as a substitute. Many female teenagers fall prey to older men, become pregnant, join the welfare system, and continue the cycle of abuse and poverty. We must teach our daughters about dating violence. Prevention will save their lives.

Helping our sons:
Sons will grow up to abuse their wives if the cycle of violence is not stopped. They will be self-destructive as well. We must teach our sons not to assault our daughters. Prevention will save our sons from the prison system.

Anger management for adolescents
Treatment for teenagers must be stated in terms of behavioral objectives. Teach both short-term and long-term goals for stopping violent behavior. Triggers that precede the violent behavior need to identified, and consequences must be applied and monitored. The root causes of domestic violence need to be presented as well.

Adolescents match the other person's emotion of anger and reflect the anger back. The anger is bounced back and forth like a ball until:
- physical fighting occurs, and someone is injured
- one person decides to stop the fight and leaves
- a third person breaks up the fight
- one person refuses to fight anymore

Christian teenagers may direct their anger at God for not stopping the abuse. They rebel against the pastor, youth pastor, church, and authority figures. They develop a distorted view of God as father and confusion about His goodness, and they quit attending youth group and Sunday school.

Peer-group counseling for adolescents

Teenagers respond better in group therapy than in individual therapy. The teen needs to know he/she is not alone and that violence occurs in other Christian homes. In group, the secret of abuse is out. At first they feel like traitors, betraying the family to strangers. They may try to protect their father/stepfather if they are in denial, but at the same time, they are glad the abuse has stopped.

Individual counseling

The power of an adult listening is encouragement for a discouraged adolescent from a violent home. It will take time for the teen to trust the counselor. He/she has learned to mistrust adults from dealing with the dynamics of an abusive home environment. As a counselor/pastor, reinforce that:
- the abuse is not the teen's fault
- the batterer is solely responsible for assaulting his wife
- if the teen was abused, he/she did not deserve it and abuse is against the law
- the teen deserves to be safe in his/her own home
- with counseling, the family can be restored
- the batterer has to accept help and stop the physical abuse before restoration can begin
- the teen is loved by many people
- the teen is valuable to God

Suicide intervention for adolescents
- Suicide is the third-leading cause of death among young people.
- Males complete suicide four times more often than females.
- Males use violent means, such as guns and hanging.
- Females use drug overdoses.

Factors associated with teenage suicide:
- family breakup
- family psychiatric problems
- alcohol and drug abuse in family
- lack of family and social support systems
- feelings of alienation and rejection
- withdrawal
- threatened or actual loss of an important relationship
- financial problems
- high academic competition
- high athletic competition
- blended families
- teen alcohol and drug abuse
- depression
- identity problems

The teen may threaten suicide for various reasons:
- anger
- depression
- revenge and punishment
- manipulation
- to end a painful situation
- a trigger or precipitating event

The removal of the father from the home may trigger a crisis for the adolescent. Police intervention is necessary if the teen runs away from home or from a domestic violence shelter.

Suicide intervention for pastors, helpers, and parents
1. Take the suicide threat seriously. Ask the teen, "Are you going to kill yourself?", "How will you kill yourself?", and "When are you going to kill yourself?"
2. Call a 24-hour crisis line for professional help.
3. Transport the teen to a 24-hour mental health crisis center or a hospital emergency room. Hospital admittance may be necessary.
4. Parents should remove guns and weapons from the home.
5. Counseling should start immediately.

Suicide Lethality Assessment

PLAN:
____ detailed plan
____ has a weapon or easy access to a gun
____ time and location have been decided

HISTORY/RISK FACTORS:
____ previous suicide attempt(s)
____ drug or alcohol abuse
____ family separation or divorce
____ has run away in the past
____ family history of alcohol/drug abuse

SYMPTOMS:
____ depression
____ apathy
____ agitation and anxiety
____ increased use of alcohol or drugs
____ increased or decreased sleep or appetite
____ continuous crying
____ lethargy
____ isolation from friends
____ severe mood swings

Teenage dating violence
- Surveys show that abuse in dating relationships is widely prevalent—about one in three females will experience violence at the hands of their boyfriends before they reach adulthood.[3]
- In self-reported data, thirty-five percent of adolescents mention at least knowing someone who experienced physical violence in a dating relationship.[4]

Intervention:

Teenagers who witness domestic violence will carry their misperceptions of marriage and male-female roles into dating relationships. Adolescents need to be taught that abusive behaviors by their boyfriend/girlfriend are crimes that are punishable offenses. Consequences must be applied and monitored. Police and parent interventions are absolutely necessary, before the violence escalates. The myth that jealousy is a trait necessary for romance needs to be dispelled, or

after the romance stage, Prince Charming may turn into a nasty toad.
- Female teenagers from divorced homes where there is not a father figure are at a greater risk. They often seek out the affections of men over twenty years of age.
- A collection of studies shows that more than fifty percent of the fathers of babies born to mothers between the ages of fifteen and seventeen are adults aged twenty or older.
- According to a California study of 47,000 births to teens in 1993, two-thirds of the babies were fathered by men who were beyond high school years.
- According to the New York Times, a Chicago study found that sixty-one percent of teenage mothers said they had been abused, often by the father of their babies.

Many teens admit that their first sexual encounters were involuntary and with an older male. Older males' preying on young teenagers is an absolute disgrace to society. We must educate our youth, and prosecute these males for statutory rape.

Prevention:
Many directors, staff, and volunteers at domestic violence shelters and coalitions speak at high schools and middle schools to educate teenagers about dating violence. Education of the teen's parents is also critical. Teachers, principals, youth leaders, and youth Sunday school teachers need to be trained to identify the signs and symptoms of dating abuse.

Women need to learn the value of completing job training or college before marriage. If they have a career, they are less likely to stay in a violent marriage and home. Helping women to become self-supporting will eliminate their poverty if they do flee from a battering husband.

It is imperative that we teach teenage males about the equality and value of teenage females. We must provide education in our churches, schools, and society about discrimination and how to change negative social, religious, and political attitudes. A female is no less valuable if she chooses a career as a mother and homemaker. The correct biblical view of the value of women to God must be taught in our youth groups and churches.

<u>Signs of a potential adolescent batterer</u>:

alcohol or drug abuse	extreme jealousy
limits her time with friends	explosive temper
forbids her to wear certain clothes	accuses her of flirting
telephones her constantly	truancy from school
wants all her attention	limits her school activities
slams his locker a lot	blames others for his anger
throws his books at her	reckless driving when angry
pressures her for sex	involved in vandalism
rebels against teachers and authority	family conflict
tells jokes that degrade women	restrains her physically
bosses her around in front of friends	criticizes her for good grades
fascination with guns/weapons	in trouble with police

<u>Television violence, musical lyrics, and the media</u>
- By the age of eighteen, the average person will have viewed about 200,000 acts of televised violence. (The American Academy of Pediatrics)

For adolescents who watch their fathers beat their mothers, television violence reinforces home life perceptions. Commercials that portray women as sexual objects, pornography magazines, and Internet pornography reinforce their warped view of the male-female role in relationships. Add violent cartoons, video games, comic books, and movies to their visual diet, and they become saturated with negative images.

Music lyrics that promote hate, rape, suicide, homicide, and rebellion are detrimental to the minds, emotions, and behaviors of our youth. Music Television (MTV) invades their bodies like a "musical cancer," eating away at values, morals, and societal norms of decency. Rock-and-roll concerts where band members perform perverted sexual acts on stage, destroy property, and encourage teens to kill their parents, plant seeds of violence in the precious minds of our youth.

Adult Christian males addicted to pornography report that the obsession started in the teenage years and progressed. Many report viewing pornography during marriage and hiding it from spouses.

NO SUICIDE CONTRACT/CHOOSE LIFE

I will not now, or ever, kill myself on purpose or even accidentally. Instead, I choose to live. I choose to ask for help. If at any time, I decide to break this contract, I will first discuss it with _____.

Your signature _____
Date _____

Witness _____
Date _____

Steps to take if I get very upset and have thoughts of suicide:

I will tell my thoughts to at least two of the following people:
- Counselor   Phone _____
- Youth leader/pastor   Phone _____
- Teacher   Phone _____
- Friend   Phone _____
- Second friend   Phone _____
- Pastor, priest, or rabbi Phone _____
- Family member (father, mother, stepparent, sister, brother, cousin, aunt, uncle, grandparent)

My personal support people are:

Name _____ Phone _____

Name _____ Phone _____

Name _____ Phone _____

I will call a teen crisis hotline if I need help:

Telephone number in my city
_____

Telephone number in my county
_____

Telephone number in my state
_____

National Hotlines:
- 1-800-448-4663
- 1-800-248-8020

Other things I can do:
_____
_____

A True Story

Cindy, a 14-year-old female from a Christian home, was brought to Christian counseling by her parents. They caught Cindy drinking alcohol. Counseling revealed that Cindy's 15-year-old boyfriend, Jeff, was abusive to her. The abuse started out as just pinching, then went to the next stage of pushing her into her school locker when he became jealous. Jeff eventually forced sex upon her. Until she attended counseling, Cindy did not know the offense was date rape and that it is a crime. Cindy felt sorry for Jeff because he was physically abused at home by his father. She felt guilty and blamed herself for the rape.

Chapter Nine

Hurting To Hope

Twelve-Step Christian Recovery Program for Children

1. Know that I am not to blame for my father or stepfather's violent behavior.
2. Know that my mother is not to blame for my father or stepfather's violent behavior.
3. Accept help from a Christian counselor. Attend family counseling.
4. Commit to daily prayer, Bible reading, and Sunday School attendance.
5. Express my feelings by talking when I am angry, sad, or frustrated.
6. Confront my father/stepfather in a safe environment. Forgive my father or stepfather. Forgive my mother for not protecting me.
7. Resolve my anger by talking, not by hitting my sisters, brothers, or friends.
8. Believe that I am a special gift from God to my parents.
9. Have fun and play sometimes.
10. Stop worrying about my parents.
11. Be nice to myself and not call myself ugly names.
12. Believe that life will get better.

Affirmation Statements:
- I am lovable.
- I am loved by many people.
- I deserve to be safe in my own home.
- I am special to Jesus.
- I am unique. There is no other person exactly like me.

Children: the Casualties of War
Statistics from the National Coalition Against Domestic Violence:
- In homes where domestic violence occurs, children are abused at a rate 1,500% higher than the national average.
- Of the children who witness domestic violence, sixty percent of the boys eventually become batterers, and fifty percent of the girls become victims.

- Seventy-three percent of male abusers were abused as children.

Statistics also state that:
- Many fathers inadvertently injure children while throwing furniture or other household objects when abusing their female partners. The youngest children sustain the most serious injuries, such as concussions, broken shoulders, and broken ribs.
- Children's lives are frequently disrupted by moves to escape domestic violence. They lose considerable school time; flee home without books, money or changes of clothing; and live in the family car when shelters are unavailable.[1]

Children who are abused by the batterer who is their father/stepfather will need counseling:

Treatment: Counseling with a Licensed Christian Child Therapist
Therapy for children:
1) Play therapy—puppets and dolls
2) Art therapy—painting, drawing, and clay

The severity and types of abuse will determine the duration of counseling. Every effort should be made to keep the child in the same home, school system, and church. It is recommend that the batterer leave the home while intervention begins. Safety for the child is the number one issue. Many times a domestic violence shelter is the safest place temporarily. The batterer must show progress in counseling before the family can be restored. Permanent safety for the children must be established before the father/stepfather can return to the home.

Children's Services will also be involved, as professionals must report suspected child abuse. The primary goal of children's protective services is to preserve the family unit intact. Through provision of appropriate supportive services, most families are able to prevent the recurrence of abuse or neglect. An estimated ninety-percent of people involved in abuse or neglect can be treated successfully. (Ohio Children's Trust Fund, *Child Abuse & Neglect: A Guide for Mandated Reporters*)

Issues to address in counseling:

suicide assessment	alcohol or drug abuse
guilt and self-blame	anger management
depression	acting out behaviors
break the cycle of violence	regression to bed wetting

nightmares/sleeping difficulties
fighting at school
low self-esteem
trust/mistrust
stealing
starting fires
physical abuse
sexual abuse/incest
emotional abuse
verbal abuse

fear of the dark
fighting with siblings
abusing siblings
poor self-image
anxiety
roles of family members
process emotions of fear
survivor guilt/grief
truancy/separation anxiety
rejection
lying/manipulating

Identifying physical child abuse:

PHYSICAL INDICATORS OF PHYSICAL ABUSE:
- unexplained, chronic bruising: face, throat, arms, buttocks, thighs, or lower back
- unexplained burns: palms, soles of feet, or abdomen
- unexplained skeletal injuries: face, skull, fracture, dislocation of arms or legs
- other injuries: welts, scars, pinch marks, missing or chipped teeth, loss of hair

BEHAVIORAL INDICATORS OF PHYSICAL ABUSE:
- extreme behaviors or withdrawal or aggression
- excessive fear of parent
- truancy or running away
- excessive crying
- hits or bites other children
- destroys other children's toys

<u>Children who are not physically abused but who witness domestic violence</u>:
- Reports by battered mothers show that eighty-seven percent of children witness the abuse.[2]
- Of children who witness their mothers being abused by their fathers, forty percent suffer with anxiety, forty-eight percent suffer depression, fifty-three percent act out with their parents, and sixty percent act out with siblings.[3]
- These children also suffer poor health, low self-esteem, poor impulse control, sleeping difficulties, and feelings of powerlessness. They are at high risk for alcohol and drug use, sexual

acting out, running away from home, isolation, loneliness, fear, and suicide.[4]

By ages six to twelve the child will have chosen a clear role, patterned after either the batterer or the victim in their family. Often the children identify with the abuser, because it is safer; they won't get hurt if they are on the batterer's side. Children who identify with the victim become more withdrawn and reclusive at this age. Others take on a "family hero" role, attempting to intervene in the acts of violence or developing an inflated sense of responsibility for the family. (*Child Advocate*, Fall 1994)

Sexual abuse/incest
It is a fact that some children are sexually abused by Christian parents/stepparents. Some children will hide this secret even during individual or group therapy. Sexual abuse in Christian homes adds another dimension of horror to domestic violence.

Identifying sexual child abuse:

PHYSICAL INDICATORS OF SEXUAL ABUSE:
- pain, irritation or bleeding of genitals or anal region
- yeast infections, urinary infections, unexplained sore throat
- torn, stained, or bloody underwear
- bruises, redness, or genital discharge

BEHAVIORAL INDICATORS OF SEXUAL ABUSE:
- bed wetting or fear of the dark
- playing with other children's genitals
- aggression, acting out, lying, stealing, or sudden changes in behavior
- separation anxiety and clinging to mother
- excessive fear of parent/stepparent

Helpers must report suspected sexual abuse to child protection agencies. Children will need a physical exam from a physician to determine injury, sexually transmitted diseases, or HIV/AIDS. Perpetrators must be held accountable in a court of law and face the consequences of prison for committing the crime of sexual abuse/incest.

While employed as a Christian therapist for a Christian counseling center, I treated many adult women who were sexually abused during childhood by their fathers who were pastors, deacons, elders, and/or men who faithfully attended church services. These women painfully hid this secret until adulthood. They desperately sought relief from the emotional torment. Most of these clients chose not to confront their abuser fathers, nor did they tell their mothers or husbands about the past traumas of sexual abuse and rape. As a minister and Christian counselor, I have counseled two types of Christian clients. Type one gives thanks to God for being with him/her during the childhood abuse; type two blames God for not stopping the childhood abuse. Sexual child abuse/incest does happen in some Christian homes. We cannot close our eyes and ears to this horrible atrocity. In the Book of Leviticus (18:6-18) the Lord spoke to Moses concerning familial incest. Verse six states, "None of you shall approach any blood relative of his to uncover nakedness; I am the Lord." The Bible condemns and speaks out against sexual abuse/incest. Religious adult men who sexually abuse their children are using power and control to dominate the bodies, minds, and souls of innocent victims.

<u>What can pastors/helpers do for the children?</u>
1. You are mandated by law to report suspected child abuse to Children's Services. They are not the enemy. They will investigate and determine the intervention for services for the child and family. Safety is the number one issue for the child.
2. Provide emotional support:
   a) assure children that the abuse is not their fault
   b) encourage them to tell the truth about the violence
   c) spend time with them
   d) pray with them and for them
   e) reinforce their strengths and positive qualities
   f) involve them in church activities
   g) explore their view of Jesus and validate Jesus' love for them
   h) give them compliments and encouraging words
3. Provide tangible items: food, clothing, shoes, school supplies, lunch money, etc.
4. Prepare them for counseling.

The unborn casualties of war:
- Between fifteen and twenty-five percent of women are battered during pregnancy. (National Coalition Against Domestic Violence)
- Domestic violence is a significant cause of miscarriage and birth defects. (March of Dimes, 1992)

- Over thirty-five percent of emergency room services provided to pregnant women are due to domestic violence. (Action Ohio)

Not all batterers abuse their pregnant wives, but some do. A survivor recently stated that her husband stopped the assaults the minute she revealed the pregnancy, only to start battering her again as soon as the baby was born. He did not physically abuse his son, but abusing someone the child loves is abuse. Abuse is when a child sees, hears, or feels family violence.

The new baby may pose a perceived threat to the marriage relationship. The batterer is jealous of anyone who receives attention from his wife. His wife will also receive extra attention from her family members and her physician. He may perceive this as loss of control over her. Some batterers force their wives to have an abortion, or they assault her until she miscarriages. The womb, like the home, should be a place of peace and safety for the unborn child. For many readers, it is hard to comprehend that some Christian men do abuse their unborn and born children. The Christian community must unite together to offer help, hope, and healing to children living in violent Christian homes.

Victims who suffer miscarriages due to abuse need to seek counseling. Human life in the womb is sacred to God. Helpers may refer the women to Christian crisis pregnancy centers for support. Batterers need to confess and ask forgiveness for the sin of murder. These men need to discuss the abuse in their Christian support/treatment/education group. May God help the abuser when he sees the wickedness of his evil ways.

<u>Elected Abortions</u>

Some batterers coerce their wives into having abortions. These women are still held accountable to God and are responsible for their actions. Both batterers and victims must confess, repent, and ask forgiveness for destroying human life. God's forgiveness is for all His children.

Abortion is the destruction of life that is created by God and created in His image. God is life. God sent His son to die on the cross for the lives of humankind—for babies in the womb; life separated from the outside environment only by layers of muscles, bone, and tissue. The Hebrew word for breath, "ruach," conveys a meaning which includes the living spirit placed within the human baby even before birth. Jesus was once in a womb. God, the giver of life, was in a womb. Life inside the womb is just as sacred as life outside the womb.

Scripture references to life in the womb:
Psalms 22:9, 10   Isaiah 29:16   Jeremiah 1:4, 5
Psalms 127:3-5   Isaiah 44:1, 2, 21, 25 Luke 1:41-44
Psalms 139:13-16   Isaiah 49:1-5

Resources:

Christian crisis pregnancy centers offer support groups for post-abortion syndrome. Call a local Christian counselor/psychologist for referrals, or check the yellow pages in your phone book.

See the directory in the back of this resource guide for a list of National Christian Crisis Pregnancy Hotline numbers.

A Note to Counselors and Shelter Staff Workers

Many shelters are starting to develop programs for children. There are videos, board/card games, and workbooks available to use for group facilitation. (See Resource section for children) Games are a therapeutic interactive tool used to help children to:
- develop problem-solving skills
- express feelings and emotions in a healthy way
- learn anger management
- build skills for personal empowerment
- build self-esteem and self-concept
- learn positive communication skills

A program for children should consist of teaching them a safety plan if the family prematurely returns to the batterer and home. This safety plan should consist of teaching children to:
- go to a neighbor's house and report the abuse
- dial 911, call the police, and/or call another family member
- not step into the middle of a fight between parents
- avoid hiding in closets or small spaces and instead to go outside and find help

Group leaders for children's groups should consist of a female and a male co-leader, so they may model equal power. Children need to know that others experience domestic violence in their homes. Family therapy can begin between the children and mother (without the father), so that the mother may be involved in the process of healing. Children may be angry with their mothers for not protecting them from the abuse and/or for leaving the home.

Issues for children

Many children at shelters suffer from separation anxiety. They are afraid to leave their mother and fear their father may hurt or kill her while they are at school. Children also suffer from guilt feelings; survivor guilt if a parent or sibling was killed, guilt for still loving the abusive parent, and guilt that they could not protect their mothers. Almost all these children feel that they are to blame for the violence. They believe that they were bad, and that's why their parents fight. Children are naturally egocentric during childhood, and they take responsibility for violence in the home. Many react with anger to every situation, because this is the major emotion they feel. Learned violence and anger will be used until they learn positive coping skills and reactions through counseling. Manipulation behaviors may be used against either parent in order to gain some control over the situation. Counselors and helpers need to address all the above issues. Shelters can also use a consultant experienced in domestic violence to set up a children's program, or the children can be referred to counselors/psychologists who specialize in child therapy.

Examples of activities to help children:
Goal—To learn about feeling and emotions
- Purchase a large roll of paper and ask children to lay on paper and draw an outline of their body. Ask them to write on the paper where feelings are located.
- Pass out a bag of M&M candies to each child. Assign an emotion to each color of candy and ask children to talk about different emotions. The red M&M candy represents anger, the blue M&M candy can represent sadness, etc.
- Purchase quick-dry plaster and have each child make a mold-mask of his/her face. Paint masks. Generate a discussion of facial expressions—what they mean and what emotion they represent.

Books about play therapy and creative activities can be purchased. Please call your state domestic violence coalition for a list of recommended videos, games, and therapeutic activities.

Discipline of children

The mothers must be taught alternative discipline methods to spanking. Physical discipline for this population is not appropriate and will only cause more emotional damage.

The Bible does not condone nor promote physical abuse as punishment. "Spare the rod and spoil the child" (Proverbs 13:24) is often misquoted, misused, and taken out of context by batterers and victims. A rod in the Old Testament is defined as a stout stick or staff approximately three to five feet long which was used by shepherds to guide, lead, and train the sheep. Shepherds did not beat and abuse the sheep with the rod/staff. The phrase "spare the rod" means that if you do not lead, nurture, train, and guide children, they will rebel against parents, authority, rules, and God. Strong's Concordance lists eighty-six scripture verses which use the word "rod." The rod in the Bible is a sign of authority. Beating children into submission is not using God-given authority—it is physical abuse. Child abuse is a sin, and a crime that is punishable by law in the United States. The Bible does not condone physical child abuse. Psalm 23:4 states, "Thy rod and Thy staff, they comfort me." Correct discipline is imperative for producing children with character, morals, values, and respect for authority. Positive parental authority is comforting to children and gives stability, which promotes trust and an emotionally and physically safe environment. Physical abuse manifests feelings of powerlessness, mistrust, fear, anger, confusion, insecurity, low self-esteem, depression, and/or rebellion in Christian children.

"And fathers, do not provoke your children to anger; but bring them up in the discipline and instruction of the Lord."
(Ephesians 6:4)

How Jesus treated children in the Bible

Jesus treated children with love, kindness, and tenderness. He healed many children, and their stories are recorded in the Bible.
- raised the ruler's daughter [Matthew 9:18,23]
- healed the gentile woman's daughter [Matthew 15:21]
- healed the epileptic boy [Matthew 17:14]
- raised a widow's son at Nain [Luke 7:11]
- healed the nobleman's son of a fever [John 4:46]

In Mark 9:36, Jesus held a child in his arms and remarked, "Whoever receives one child like this in My name receives me." In Mark 9:42, Jesus said, "And whoever causes one of these little ones who believe to stumble, it would be better for him if, with a heavy millstone hung around his neck, he had been cast into the sea."

True Story

Ginger arrived at the domestic violence shelter with her four children. Her ten year-old son was showing signs of anger and rebellion due to the constant verbal abuse and criticism from his stepfather. Three years of emotional/verbal abuse was taking toil on Ginger as well as the four children. After her first marriage ended due to emotional/verbal abuse, Ginger decided to only marry a Christian man who attended church, prayed and read the Bible. Ginger met Brad at a church and shortly married him. He possessed all the qualities she wanted in a husband. Brad read his Bible every night. Ginger was shocked when the emotional/verbal abuse started immediately after the wedding. Brad was more abusive than her first husband. Ginger did not have a job, a home, or any money. Her safety net was welfare and public housing.

Chapter Ten

Marital Restoration

Recipe for reconciliation
    2 people who want to reconcile
    1 almighty God
    2 relationships with the Holy Spirit
    1 Christian counselor and/or pastor
    1 Christian support group for male batterers
    Support from church family
    Support from relatives & friends
    Bible and prayer and spiritual growth
    Communication
    Commitment
    Confession and repentance and forgiveness
    Courage
    Faith

Put the above ingredients into your relationship, and stir well.

Marital counseling
<u>Guidelines for Counseling Men</u>:
A. Teach men that masculinity and emotions are compatible. Showing emotions does not portray weakness and powerlessness.
B. Men are usually visual and/or "hands-on" learners. Visual learners need to see concrete examples. Use a marker board, videos, handouts, and visual aids in sessions.
C. Give men concrete assignments outside of counseling:
    1. Watch one video on communication skills
    2. Fill out handouts on counseling topics
    3. Give your wife two compliments and two hugs each day
D. Ask men to set cognitive behavioral goals for counseling. Instruct them to break down goals into small, achievable steps.

Guidelines for Counseling Women:
  A. Teach women to balance emotions with reasoning when discussing decision-making skills. Women are more aware of feelings than thoughts and behaviors.
  B. Instruct women on their value to God by using examples of women in the New Testament.
  C. Encourage women to give verbal examples and not to assume that men can read minds.
  D. Ask women to set cognitive, behavioral, and spiritual goals for counseling.

Victims and Batterers

Batterers have many positive qualities. Many are good providers, fathers, and workers in the church and community. Many have successful careers and are highly respected by their peers.

Victims are imperfect human beings and not saints. They make mistakes and commit sinful behaviors; the point is that they do not deserve to be abused for any reason.

There are conflict and problems in every marriage, but not all husbands resort to physical violence. The husband who abuses brings the violence into the marriage. He would batter whomever he married.

Marriage restoration

This resource guide is written for married couples. God does not advocate cohabitation. Christian women who are living with their boyfriends without the sanctity of marriage will reap the consequences. They must confess, repent, and change their lifestyle so their prayers will not be hindered.

Domestic violence counselors recommend six to eighteen months of separation for the victim and batterer before they reunite. This time period can vary based on the individual situation. If couple counseling is begun prematurely, the victim will be intimidated by her abuser/husband. She will return to the marriage only to be victimized again. The severity of the physical abuse is also a variable. The more severe the assault, the longer it takes to heal and restore the marriage.

The batterer needs to be asked this question in the first session, "Do you want the violence to stop?" If his answer is "no," then do not proceed with marital counseling. Refer him back to the male support/treatment/education group and recommend continued separation for the wife.

The first goal of marital counseling for the violence-prone husband is the prevention of further violence. Assess the following:
- strengths of the couple
- existing resources available
- interventions that worked for them in the past
- how they solved problems in the past without violence
- positive qualities about the relationship
- their common ground
- current coping skills

Some studies suggest that both men and women physically assault each other; but men, the stronger of the sexes, inflict more severe injuries. It is rare to find a Christian wife who assaults her husband, even in self-defense.

Couple counseling can begin ONLY after the husband has attended a Christian support/ treatment/education group for male batterers and pastoral/Christian therapy. Do not initiate marital counseling until the husband has met certain requirements—to attempt restoration prematurely will put the woman in danger. If the wife reveals the abuse in marital counseling, her husband will beat her when they leave your office. If she does not reveal the abuse, the counseling is useless. The vast majority of professional mental health counselors who specialize in domestic violence cases also advise this method. The following criteria needs to be met by the abuser first:

1. He sincerely admits he is solely responsible for physically assaulting his wife.
2. He is repentant and sorry.
3. He has asked forgiveness of God.
4. He is ready to change.
5. He has learned anger management skills.
6. He has a male accountability partner.
7. He is ready to ask his wife to forgive him.
8. He has attended Christian counseling for a minimum of six months and shows progress.
9. He understands the root causes of power and control issues.
10. He understands God's truth about the true meaning of submission in the scripture.

A team approach to couple counseling is recommended—a male and female counselor or a pastor and his wife. A female counselor without a male partner is a threat to the recovering male batterer.

Short- and Long-term Goals of Couple Counseling
1. Restoration of marriage
2. Conflict resolution
3. Communication skills
4. Establish prayer and Bible reading together as a couple
5. Reinforce anger management skills
6. Put God in marriage
7. Husband to become spiritual leader of the home
8. Establish regular church attendance
9. Teach couple to have fun with humor
10. Prepare couple for family counseling for restoration of children
11. Set practice dates for couple to be alone together
12. Establish intimacy and renewal of sexual relations
13. Confirm salvation and rededication of their lives to Jesus
14. Teach coping skills and stress reduction
15. Redefine distorted marital expectations and roles of husband/wife
16. Explore equal power and equal submission in marriage
17. Explore financial budgets or refer to a financial counselor

Structuring the Counseling Sessions
1st session—set ground rules:
- No yelling
- No name calling
- No physical assaulting
- No threatening
- No blaming
- Time-out if either person shows signs of anger escalation
- No interrupting the other person
- No degrading of in-laws
- No shaming
- No sarcastic humor
- No pointing fingers or rolling eyes (nonverbal body language)
- Attack problems, not each other

If these rules can not be followed, the session should be terminated and another appointment date set for the future. The man needs to process his behaviors at his next support/treatment/education group meeting or meet with his accountability partner. Allow the wife to leave several minutes before the husband does to avoid conflict in your parking lot. Call the police immediately if the husband assaults his wife in your office!

Prayer:
1. Start each session with prayer. Pray for a peaceful session to set the mood. Ask for guidance from the Holy Spirit.
2. Prayers can be used in the middle of the session if the couple is headed toward the danger zone of negative conflict escalation.
3. Close with prayer. Ask each person for prayer requests for the marriage.
4. Assign each person daily prayers:
    a) Both should pray every day for healing, understanding, encouragement, truth, and honesty for self, mate, and family.
    b) Assign daily Bible scriptures—one Psalm every morning and one Proverb every night. Increase scripture as they make progress. Do not overwhelm them with too many scriptures. Eventually you may assign the couple to read the Song of Solomon together.
    c) Eventually the couple can practice praying out loud together at the close of the sessions.

Homework assignments:
- Videos to watch together about family violence (see Resource Section for recommendations)
- Hand-outs for written exercises (see Tool Section)
- Practice of skills and techniques

Areas to address in counseling:
1. Conflict resolution
    a) How to disagree without violence
    b) How to communicate: reading nonverbal body language and verbal language
    c) Communication patterns we learned from our parent(s)
    d) "I" and "you" statements

2. Forgiveness issues
    a) Husband needs to verbally ask for forgiveness
    b) Wife needs to confront husband about past abuse
    c) Wife needs to verbally forgive husband
    d) Re-establish trust

NOTE: The wife needs to resolve her anger, bitterness, and resentment towards her husband before confronting him. Confrontation is for healing purposes, not for blaming, shaming, or humiliating her husband. Do not attempt confrontation prematurely in couple counseling. Pray, and ask for Holy Spirit guidance. If the abuser is not prepared, he could refuse to apologize or confess, and the wife may be victimized again. The choice as to whether to confront should always be hers. The possible benefits and dangers of confrontation of past abuse should be addressed first. The team counselors can meet with the husband/wife individually before this part of healing is initiated. The benefits of confrontation include facing fears, processing painful emotions, closing the door on the past, and moving to the next stage of healing.

The wife needs to know that forgiveness is not accomplished just by voicing the words. It is a continuous, ongoing process. She may be tempted to pull out her "arsenal of pain" weapons—past injuries, bitterness, and resentment. She may find herself shooting arrows of blame and shame at her husband. This is a critical stage in the healing of a relationship. She can take advantage of her husband's surrender and sabotage him, or she can seek the compassion of the Holy Spirit and try to see Jesus in her husband. She is responsible for her reactions and responses.

Intimacy issues
- Emotional aspects of physical intimacy
- Renewal of sexual relations
- Future sexual relations upon the consent of both parties–no forced sex, verbal manipulation, or threats
- Renewal of wedding vows after healing is completed—a ceremony with your pastor would be appropriate if both wife and husband are in agreement.

The "C's" of marriage:

Christ-centered	compassionate	courage
committed	companionship	consistency
communication	covenant	church
caring	cuddling	considerate
compliments	common ground	compromise

If the abusive husband will not stop the physical violence and accept intervention, then there are other options. If he is confronted by the pastor, church board members, police and/or court systems and still refuses counseling, then the wife has other options. I do not advocate divorce, but I do advocate safety for the wife. The marriage covenant has already been broken by his violence. Battered Christian women need to know that we live in the age of grace, and divorce will not send them to hell. Christians have eternal security in Christ and eternal life in heaven. But divorce should be the last resort.

Options:
- permanent legal separation without divorce
- divorce without remarriage, if the husband did not commit adultery
- divorce with remarriage, if the husband committed adultery (Matthew 19:9)
- divorce if the husband is not a Christian and abandons the family, and remarriage (1 Corinthians 7:15)

Chuck Swindoll wrote in his book, *Strike the Original Match*: "It is unrealistic and unfair to think regardless of sure danger and possible loss of life, a godly mate and helpless children should subject themselves to brutality and other forms of extreme mistreatment. At that point, commitment to Christ supersedes all principles in a home. I am not advocating divorce...but I do suggest restraint and safety via a separation..."[1]

As an ordained minister, I know this is an extremely serious issue. I believe in the restoration of marriages and God's families, and I know what the Bible teaches about divorce. Each wife needs to seek the grace of God and make her own decisions. I do not make these decisions for the women to whom I minister.

I know, however, from years of experience working with Christian battered women, that there are some marriages that cannot be reconciled—the husband will not stop the physical abuse. In some cases, the husband stops the physical abuse but continues and even increases the emotional, verbal, and spiritual abuse. The institution of marriage does not take precedence over the life or death issues of battered women.

"He (the Lord) no longer regards the offering or accepts it with favor from your hand. Yet you say, "For what reason?" Because the Lord has been a witness between you and the wife of your youth, against whom you have dealt treacherously, though she is your companion and your wife by covenant.

(Malachi 2:13-14)

Psalm 7:12-16 states what will happen to a violent man who does not repent:

> "If a man does not repent, he will sharpen his sword;
> he has bent his bow and made it ready.
> He has also prepared for himself deadly weapons.
> He makes his arrows fiery shafts.
> Behold, he travails with wickedness,
> and he conceives mischief, and brings forth falsehood.
> He has dug a pit and hollowed out,
> and has fallen into the hole which he made.
> His mischief will return upon his own head,
> and his violence will descend upon his own plate."

The Song of Solomon represents the love between Christian husbands and wives. This tender analogy also represents the love God (the Bridegroom) has for His church (the Bride). Domestic violence defiles the purpose of marriage and destroys the relationship.

The Song of Solomon
[Chapter 2:1-10]

Bride: "I am the rose of Sharon, the lily of the valleys."

Bridegroom: "Like a lily among the thorns, so is my darling among the maidens."

Bride: "Like an apple tree among the trees of the forest, so is my beloved among the young men. In his shade I took great delight and sat down, and his fruit was sweet to my taste. He has brought me to his banquet hall, and his banner over me is love. Sustain me with raisin cakes, refresh me with apples, because I am lovesick. Let his left hand be under my head and his right hand embrace me."

Bridegroom: "I adjure you, O daughters of Jerusalem, by the gazelles or by the hinds of the field, that you will not arouse or awaken my love, until she pleases."

Bride: "Listen! My beloved! Behold, he is coming, climbing on the mountains, leaping on the hills! My beloved is like a gazelle or a young stag. Behold, he is standing behind our wall, he is looking through the windows, he is peering through the lattice. My beloved responded and said to me, 'Arise, my darling, my beautiful one, and come along. For behold, the winter is past, the rain is over and gone. The flowers have already appeared in the land; the time has arrived for pruning the vines, and the voice of the turtledove has been heard in our land. The fig tree has ripened its figs, and the vines in blossom have given forth their fragrance. Arise my darling, my beautiful one, and come along! O my dove, in the clefts of the rock, in the secret place of the steep pathway, let me see your form, let me hear your voice; for your voice is sweet, and your form is lovely.'"

"Heavenly Father, I pray for healing of marital relationship and Christian marriages. Speak to husbands through the Song of Solomon and use your word to transform them into godly men of honor in their homes. Holy Spirit show them the truth. In Jesus' name. Amen."

Putting the Pieces of Your Family Back Together

"The ruin of a nation begins at home."
Ashanti Proverb

The families in the Bible are continually "putting the pieces back together." The Bible is a manual for family restoration.

It is important to state again that family restoration should begin only after the batterer has attended a Christian support/ treatment/ education group for male batterers, individual Christian/pastoral counseling, and marital counseling. Do not initiate family counseling prematurely, due to safety concerns for the children. Recommendations from the support group leader and counselor/pastor are required. If treatment is court ordered, progress should be reported to the designated person.

<u>Issues to address</u>:
- forgiveness for past abuse
- children's fear that he may abuse again
- safety plan and police intervention
- relapse of batterer into violence

- goals for the future
- conflict resolution skills
- communication skills
- nonphysical discipline
- reading the Bible together as a family
- praying together
- weekly family meetings
- planning fun activities

The family can be assigned short segments of time together. The time can increase as the husband shows he is capable of using his learned skills of anger management. Once again, the duration of counseling depends on several factors:

- past severity of physical abuse to the wife
- past physical abuse to children
- past verbal, emotional, or sexual abuse of children
- involvement of Children's Services
- sobriety and treatment, if alcohol and drugs are a problem
- mental illness and treatment/medication
- past head trauma and treatment/medication

If Children's Services is involved, due to neglect or abuse of the children, they will also provide intervention and decide when the husband can return to the home. If the children were temporarily placed in foster care, a case manager will set guidelines and requirements for reconciliation.

> **"Fathers, do not exasperate your children:
> instead, bring them up in the training
> and instruction of the Lord."
> (Ephesians 6:4)**

The following is a true story. The names have been changed for privacy and protection.

Kim and Robert were married for fifteen years. They both were active in their church. Robert taught Sunday school. Robert physically, emotionally, verbally, spiritually, economically, and sexually abused Kim during most of the marriage. He often threatened to kill Kim if she ever left him. He would flash a gun to prove it. Kim would not leave him because of her Christian character and her belief in permanent wedding vows. Kim eventually attended therapy for her depression. Her childhood secret was sexual abuse by her father and brother. Their teenage adopted daughter revealed the secret of sexual abuse by Robert. She also contracted a sexually transmitted disease from Robert—proof that he had committed adultery.

Robert confessed, repented, and asked forgiveness before the church congregation. He wanted his marriage and family to be reconciled, but it was too late—Robert was convicted and sent to prison for sexual abuse. He suffered the earthly consequences of his crime: he lost his wife, family, job, house, and freedom. This marriage covenant could not be restored. Divorce was Kim's solution. Counseling in prison revealed Robert's childhood secret—sexual abuse by an older male. Victims of childhood abuse often marry other victims.

The truth has set Robert free, and he can now heal through Jesus Christ. Kim is remarried. Her home is now peaceful and safe. She praises the Lord for her escape from her abusive marriage. Her daughter is still healing. Her son is still healing. God can take a tragedy and use it for His glory. Both Kim and Robert are reconciled to God but not to each other. God can still use both of them in His kingdom.

Chapter Eleven

Prevention of Domestic Violence

What Can the Church Do?

<u>For Married Adults</u>:
1. Marriage seminars and retreats
2. Resources in church libraries about family violence: books, videos, manuals, etc.
3. Schedule special speakers on topics such as communications, conflict resolution, marriage building, etc.
4. Address the topic of domestic violence in men's groups.
5. Address the topic of abuse in women's groups.
6. Accountability groups for men and women
7. Teach the correct biblical view of submission.

<u>For Singles</u>:
1. Premarital counseling and a two-year engagement period before marriage
2. Special speakers for singles on topics such as choosing a mate, spotting a potential batterer, how to do a police check before a relationship turns into serious dating, etc.
3. Resources in church libraries for singles: books, videos, resource guides, etc.

<u>For Teenagers</u>:
1. Education about dating violence and date rape in youth group meetings
2. Teach the signs of a potential abuser.
3. Show videos on family violence and teenage dating violence.
4. Use available teenage curricula and workbooks.
5. Schedule as a guest speaker a teenager who recovered from dating violence.

<u>For Pastors</u>:
1. Preach from the pulpit on domestic violence; intervention and prevention. Include victims and abusers in public prayers.

2. Become a board member of your local coalition against domestic violence.
3. Offer meeting space in your church to local domestic violence coalitions.
4. Provide brochures in the church about community services for victims, batterers, and children.
5. Ask your church board, deacons, and Sunday School teachers to attend seminars about domestic violence prevention.
6. Teach the equality of women and mutual submission.
7. Portray how Jesus treated his female followers in the scriptures.
8. Teach both the male and female traits of Jesus.
9. Teach that domestic violence is a sin against God.
10. In rural communities, if no shelter exists, join with local churches to establish a shelter.
11. Encourage women to be on the church board and hold positions of office in the church.

For The Christian Community:
1. Believe the victims.
2. Pray for the victims, children, and batterers.
3. Develop a prison ministry for batterers. These men will eventually be released. Offer them Jesus, hope, and healing
4. Christian men, unite and mentor the batterers.
5. Church boards, hold your pastors, deacons, elders, and men accountable if they are batterers.
6. Volunteer your time at your local domestic violence shelter.
7. Start prevention programs in your church.
8. Attend local meetings about domestic violence.
9. Use referrals to Christian counselors for victims and batterers.
10. Accompany the victims to court, and hold batterers accountable for their violent behaviors.

The following groups can be educated on the prevention of domestic violence:

Faith-Based Education System
High schools and after school programs
Colleges and universities
Daycare programs

Faith-Based Men's Ministries
Promise Keepers
T.D. Jakes Manpower Seminars

Faith-Based Social Services
Campus Crusade for Christ
Youth for Christ
Prison Ministries
Pregnancy Distress Centers
Christian Counseling Centers

Faith-Based Professionals
Lawyers
Physicians and nurses
Dentists
Chaplains

Faith-Based Media
Radio/Talk Radio
Television, local and national
Magazines and newspapers
Internet/World Wide Web

Prevention of Domestic Violence in our Christian Homes

How do we prevent domestic violence? By changing the human heart. Jesus came to earth to help people change internally. When people change, then domestic violence will change. All the social and educational programs in the world will not change the human heart–the change must be within the person. The change comes only from accepting Jesus Christ as Lord and Savior. The change comes from experiencing a true conversion by the Holy Spirit. Christian men who batter must seek a right relationship with the God of the Bible. America needs to embrace again the Biblical principles upon which she was founded; only then will we see a permanent change in the violence in our homes, families, and nation.

Satan knows that a house divided against itself will not stand. He creates chaos in Christian homes to prevent couples and families from spreading the Gospel. Broken and wounded families cannot lead others into God's kingdom. Satan will do anything to discredit their testimony and witnessing for Christ. A church congregation is only as healthy as the families who sit in the pews each week. Jesus is the answer to the problem of domestic violence in society and in our Christian homes.

Domestic violence is a spiritual problem as well, and the church must deal with it! (Ephesians 6:12) Christians cannot look to the world and secular shelters for answers to spiritual problems and domestic/demoniac violence.

Our communities do need to work together to address the prevention of domestic violence. We need to make external changes as well as internal changes, including:
- more domestic violence shelters, both secular and Christian
- transitional houses for male batterers

- improved police protection and intervention
- quick arrests and consequences for batterers
- improved legal system
- referrals to social workers and counselors
- court-ordered treatment for the offenders
- more public housing for women and children who leave a batter who will not stop the abuse
- education for physicians and nurses about injuries to battered women
- education about dating violence for our youth
- exposure from the media about the crime of domestic violence
- help from social agencies
- more treatment programs through the churches
- more prison programs that address treatment for batterers
- community collaboration of agencies and churches
- men and women working together to promote the value of women
- men standing together to send a message that domestic violence will not be tolerated

How Religious and Secular Communities Can Work Together

<u>How can pastors, priests, and rabbis help women of faith at secular shelters?</u>
- Build a relationship with the director, board, and staff members at the shelters
- Offer to speak at shelters about religious issues clarifying that religion and the Bible do not condone domestic violence to women, children, or men.
- Provide Bibles, religious videos, and books.
- Offer transportation to church services.
- Give the director a list of pastors' names and numbers in the community.
- Give the director a referral list for Christian counselors.
- Ask for brochures to display at your church.
- Invite shelter workers to present workshops for your congregation.
- Support the shelter financially or help with fund-raisers.
- Call the victims from your church while they are at shelters.

How can workers at secular shelters help women of faith who are victims?

- Ask her about her faith, church family, and spiritual needs.
- Call a designated pastor, rabbi, or priest upon her request (establish a relationship with them in advance so you will know their doctrine and beliefs about marital abuse).
- Take her religious concerns seriously when she talks about divorce and her spiritual values.
- Make contact with religious counseling agencies (Christian counselors, Christian inpatient psychiatric hospitals, Jewish Family Services, Lutheran Social Services, Catholic Community Services, etc.).
- Offer to speak to churches about the services of secular shelters.
- Offer educational resources to churches and public libraries.
- Develop a relationship with religious leaders in the community.
- Educate your staff about religious issues and values concerning divorce.
- Teach the view that women of faith do not deserve to be abused and anyone who condones marital violence is wrong.
- Keep Bibles at the shelter for the Christian women.

How can religious domestic violence shelters and secular shelters build partnerships?

- Attend joint training workshops.
- Share videos, books, and educational resources.
- Establish a committee comprised of shelter workers, pastors, rabbis, priests, and congregational members.
- Make referrals to victims based upon their spiritual values (some victims will feel more secure in a religious shelter, while others will prefer a secular shelter).

Secular shelters receive state and federal funding; therefore they are limited in what religious activities can be promoted. The staff members can help each individual victim with her spiritual concerns and needs.

Secular shelters and the religious community often mistrust each other due to miscommunication and different philosophies. In the past, the church has often been silent about domestic violence in Christian families, and many even encouraged the victims to return to violent homes. More and more churches are now recognizing the seriousness of domestic violence and offering referrals and support groups. Oftentimes secular shelters are viewed as promoting divorce and the breakup of the family without giving restoration a chance first. The number one goal of both organizations should be safety for the women and children. Together, the religious and secular community agencies can form a powerful team. We can communicate and work together to help the victims, batterers, and children.

Scriptures to give to Christian battered women when they seek safety at secular shelters.

Matthew 10:36
And a man's enemies will be the members of his household.

Malachi 2:13
And this is another thing you do; you cover the altar of the Lord with tears, with weeping, and with groaning, because He no longer regards the offering or accepts it with favor from your hand. Yet you say, "For what reason?" Because the Lord has been a witness between you and the wife of your youth, against whom you have dealt treacherously, though she is your companion and your wife by covenant.

2 Timothy 3:1-7
But realize this, that in the last days difficult times will come. For men will be lovers of self, lovers of money, boastful, arrogant, revilers, disobedient to parents, ungrateful, unholy, unloving, irreconcilable, malicious, gossips, without self-control, brutal, haters of good, treacherous, reckless, conceited, lovers of pleasure rather than lovers of God; holding to a form of godliness, although they have denied its power; and avoid such men as these. For among them are those who enter households and captivate weak women weighted down with sins, led on by various impulses, always learning and never able to come to the knowledge of the truth.

1 Peter 3:7
You husbands likewise, live with your wives in an understanding way, as with a weaker vessel, since she is a woman; and grant her honor as a fellow heir of the grace of life, so that your prayers may not be hindered.

Ephesians 5:28-29
So husbands ought also to love their own wives as their own bodies. He who loves his own wife loves himself; for no one ever hated his own flesh, but nourishes and cherishes it, just as Christ also does the church.

Psalm 18:48
He delivers me from my enemies; surely Thou dost lift me above those who rise against me; Thou dost rescue me from the violent man.

Psalm 30:5b
Weeping may last for the night, but a shout of joy comes in the morning.

Psalm 31:20
Thou dost hide them in the secret place of thy presence from the conspiracies of man; Thou dost keep them secretly in a shelter from the strife of tongues.

Psalm 72:12-14
He will rescue their life from oppression and violence; and their blood will be precious in His sight.

How Parents, Relatives, & Friends Can Help Victims

Parents, relatives, and friends are the indirect victims of domestic violence. They are unsure of what to do and how to help. They feel so helpless when the victim will not leave the batterer. He may force her to choose between her parents or him. Quick intervention could save her life.

Options:

1. If you witness him physically abusing her, call the police. Encourage her to call police. Document all incidents.
2. If he is abusing your grandchildren, call and report the abuse to Children's Services.
3. Parents and friends need to develop a safety plan if she decides to leave him. He may threaten you and attempt to do you bodily harm.
4. Be aware of community resources and domestic violence shelters in your area and share the information with her.
5. Allow her to hide her emergency kit at your home where the batterer will not find it.

6. Let her know she can stay with you if she leaves him.
7. Help her to relocate to another town or state if necessary.
8. Educate her about the laws and statistics. Discuss police intervention.
9. Keep brochures, books, and videos about domestic violence in your home and encourage her to review them when she visits you.
10. Assist her in looking at her options.
11. Encourage her to attend support group meetings for battered women. Go to the meetings with her.
12. Encourage her to talk to their pastor.
13. Take pictures of her injuries. Keep the pictures hidden at your house.

Signs of Domestic Violence in a Marriage

1. He limits their family visits to holidays and occasional evenings.
2. These visits may end abruptly with his temper tantrums.
3. He criticizes her in public.
4. She often looks sad and withdrawn.
5. She starts having many appointments with the doctor.
6. She wears long-sleeved shirts, even in the summer—to hide the bruises.
7. Her make-up may appear to be caked on her face at times—to hide facial bruises.
8. Her style of clothing starts to change. She now wears modest, unflattering outfits.
9. She abruptly quits the job she enjoyed for no apparent reason.
10. They sell their second car. He wants her to be at home.
11. He barks orders and she instantly obeys.
12. She is constantly apologizing for his rude behaviors.
13. He may move her to another town or state. He says it's to better the family. What he is doing is isolating her from contact with family and friends.
14. She tells lies to keep the abuse a secret.

Quick intervention is the best way to help her. Do not wait if you suspect abuse. Talk to her immediately. Take action but only after you seek information from a professional counselor and/or a domestic violence shelter.

Chapter Twelve

Poetry Therapy

The Power of Poetry

Written words are powerful. The words of the Bible are powerful. The Book of Psalms brings comfort and inspiration when we are in a spiritual valley. Poetry is powerful, especially if the poems were inspired by the Holy Spirit. Poetry is therapeutic to the healing process for many.

The content of poetry can be a balm for our emotional wounds. Soothing words can comfort us in times of deepest sorrow. Words are healing—and words are revealing. Words help us confess—words help us express. Words bring tears—words calm our fears. Words written in God's truth bring light to the darkest part of our souls.

<u>Clergy, Counselors, and Helpers</u>:

Please use these poems as you minister to victims of domestic violence. Christian women need to know that there are others who have walked in their shoes, that they are not alone.

<u>Christian Victims</u>:

At one time I, too, felt hopeless and helpless. I am now a victor in Jesus Christ. You can be a victor, too. It is my prayer that these poems will bring hope, courage, and compassion to your broken hearts and broken homes.

What follows are a few examples of poetry that expresses the deepest emotion of that writer. It is an outlet for healing and a method for putting thoughts and feelings into words.

Until Death Do Us Part

Husband and Wife, "Until death do you part",
The Groom heard these words and took them to heart.

The Groom shouted, "Submission! Submit I say!"
"I'm the head of the house. God made it that way!"

The Groom said, "Quit your job, and stay home all day.
Don't talk on the phone, and do what I say!"

The Groom hit her, he beat her, he broke her bones,
Then he quoted from the Bible and ripped out the phone.

The Bride ran to her family and they gave her advice,
"You said 'I do,' and now you pay the price."

The Bride ran to the Church, and they told her to pray,
Keep the house cleaner and try to obey.

The Bride went to a Christian counselor for relief from the pain, He said, "Forgive him, and go back again."

The Bride went to the hospital, bloodied and sore;
The Groom by her side said, "She ran into a door."

One night in a rage he threw her against a wall,
He beat her to death by crushing her skull.

The Bride cried out to the Heavenly Father above,
"I didn't want bruises. I only wanted love."

The Father in Heaven opened up His book and with a long pause...
He said, "When I wrote 'until death do you part,' I meant by a natural cause."

Middle Class Domestic Violence

Daddy's hitting Mommy once again,
She tries to run but he always wins.

The children run to their rooms and weep,
They'll cry until they fall asleep.

The pillows are wet with their tears,
Screams and nightmares reveal their fears.

He gives her flowers after the fight,
He says, "I'm sorry, it will be all right."

She hides the bruises—black and blue,
He made by hitting her with his shoe.

He blames the beer when he gets mad.
He reminds her of her dad.

Then he will clean the house and wash all the dishes,
Treat her like a queen and grant all her wishes.

He only beats her every 90 days,
The other 89—that's why she stays.

He is loving, caring, and kind,
Except when alcohol is on his mind.

He takes them to church every Sunday,
They sing, laugh, and have a fun day.

They live in a big house on the hill,
He provides well and pays the bills.

She reads her Bible and prays each night,
Asking God to make her a better wife.

Hearts Held Hostage

For better or for worse,
A blessing or a curse?
The wedding vow is broken,
The silence of violence unspoken.

Thorn in my side,
A secret to hide.
Is it from Satan,
Or is it my pride?

A cross I must carry,
Or shame I must bury?
Spiritual oppression,
Or chemical depression?

It is caused by sin,
Or pain from within?
I need to be healed,
The root cause revealed.

Holy Spirit, where did it start?
Take me back to the ache in my heart.
Show me the memories of pain and despair,
Help me to forgive with Jesus and prayer.

Broken Covenant

Marital rites,
Violent fights

Beautiful union,
Spilled communion

Wedding vows,
Sacred cows

For better or worse,
A blessing or curse

Love, honor, and obey,
Hate, disgrace, and decay

To love and to cherish,
To hurt and to perish

The Cycle

He hits his wife, that's what men do.
He saw his father hit his mom, too.

He hits his kids when they don't obey.
His dad hit him 'most every day.

To his small son he replies, "Don't you know—boys don't cry.
Stand up straight and dry your eyes."

His teenage son goes on a date,
And hits his girlfriend if she is late.

His teenage daughter full of hate,
Will tolerate abuse in a mate.

The men in the family "Keep the women in line."
They don't know domestic violence is a crime.

Unholy Matrimony

Filled with violence and despair,
Unholy Matrimony
A cross I must bear?
Unholy Matrimony
Sadness, pain, and tears,
Unholy Matrimony
The loud silence of my fears.

Holy Matrimony

Filled with kindness and love,
Holy Matrimony
Created from God above,
Holy Matrimony
Based on intimacy and trust,
Holy Matrimony
A gift from God to us.

Poisoned Passion

In his jealous rage he calls me a whore,
He says I'm unfaithful and rotten to the core.

He says I'm ugly, stupid, and fat,
No other man would want me like that.

When we go to a party, I stick close by his side,
I keep my eyes down and avoid other men's eyes.

I can't wear make-up, he calls it a sin.
If my pants are too tight, I'm trying to attract other men.

Fifty questions at the end of every day,
Who did I talk to? What did they say?

He tells me I'm crazy and going insane,
I start to believe him–unaware of his game.

I speak no opinions of my own,
I make no decisions in my home.

He wants sex on demand,
He says that's part of God's plan.

He lives for the day of total control,
He wants to dominate my mind, heart, and soul.

His ego he feeds on marital power,
All my energy he tries to devour.

I am numb–no more tears,
My only emotion is my fear.

His charming smile he shows the town,
Out in public he acts the clown.

As I keep this secret I feel so alone,
I am a prisoner in my home.

Seven years of brainwashing by this man,
Am I strong enough to make a stand?

I walk on eggshells day and night,
I make my choice–divorce or suicide?

Will the church understand?
I will take no more abuse from this man.

I go to court to save my life,
No more pain–no more strife.

Thank you, Jesus, I say instead,
I'd rather be divorced than dead.

Not Generational Welfare

There is a small segment of the population that needs to be recognized for its courage. This article is dedicated to the Christian single moms who temporarily receive public assistance (welfare), but who desire a better life for themselves and their children. These women are on welfare because they left a violent marriage. They left to save their lives and the lives of their children.

<u>Who We Are Not</u>

The title describes who we are not. We are not generational welfare recipients. We do not accept welfare as a permanent way of living. Our parents did not receive public assistance. We are not lazy bums, as some would stereotype. We do not sit in front of the television all day and watch soap operas while eating chocolate bon-bons. We are not alcoholics or drug addicts. We do not have multiple births just to increase our monthly welfare checks. We do not cheat the system. We are not proud to be on welfare. We are not illiterate. We are not psychotic. We do not hang out in bars and pick up men. We do not have body odor from not taking baths. We do not spend our food stamps on prime rib. We do not have lice. We do not abuse our children. We do not eat out in restaurants every night. We do not spend our welfare checks on lottery tickets, cigarettes, and beer. We are not being punished by God because we are divorced.

<u>Who We Are</u>

We are survivors. We are single parents. We are women who made wrong choices by marrying abusive men. We are women who do not receive child support or who receive very little child support. We are good mothers. We love our children. We are intelligent. We are struggling to provide a better life for our children. We are trying to become self-sufficient. We are women with values and morals. We are citizens of the United States of America. We keep our houses clean. We can read and write. We have a driver's license. We attend church. We read our Bibles. We are sinners saved by grace, like every other Christian. We are proud that we are trying to change our situation. We are Christians. Christians can receive public assistance and still go to Heaven.

<u>How We Do Not Deserve to be Treated</u>

We do not deserve to be treated like outcasts of American society. We do not deserve shunning from our church families or pastors. We do not deserve to be criticized and called names. We do not deserve looks of disgust from the cashiers at the grocery stores when we use our food stamps. We do not deserve to be stereotyped. Our children do not deserve to be ridiculed because they receive free school lunches.

How We Deserve to be Treated

We deserve to be treated with respect. We are to be commended for raising our children with Christian values. We deserve a chance to make our lives better. We need to be encouraged by our church families and our pastors. We deserve an opportunity to pursue a college education. Education is one key to our empowerment. The gaining of knowledge and information allows us to make better future decisions. We will then be able to find jobs that will pay the rent, put food on our tables, and provide medical insurance. We deserve help from the child support enforcement agencies.

How Did We End Up On Welfare?

Low self-esteem + Marriage + Abusive Husband + Children + Divorce + No Child Support + No Medical Benefits + No Job Skills = WELFARE.

The scenario is the same for many women trapped in the welfare system. We made poor choices, and we suffer the consequences of our choices. Unfortunately, our children also suffer. Many women receiving public assistance have domestic violence in their pasts. Even though we chose to marry him, we did not choose to be abused. We were not responsible for his violent behavior. We saved our lives by leaving. We broke the cycle of abuse for ourselves and for our children. There is a war being fought in many families in America. It is called domestic violence. When women win the war and end the violent marriage, they face another battle—the battle to collect child support. They face the battle of poverty.

When we played house as little girls, we did not pretend to be moms on welfare. We did not discuss poverty at our tea parties. We never said, "When I grow up, I want to be on welfare". Welfare was not our dream. It became our nightmare. Then it became the hope for our future. Without welfare we would not be where we are today: SELF-SUFFICIENT.

Do we blame the abusive husband? Do we blame the police and/or legal system? Do we blame the child support enforcement agency for not trying harder to collect our support payments? Do we blame our dysfunctional families of origin? Do we blame our culture? Do we blame our society? Do we blame God? Not anymore. Blame does not put food on the table. We swallow what is left of our pride and visit the Human Services Department with our heads down and our hands out. We sigh with relief when we reach into our mailboxes and pull out our food stamps, knowing our children will eat for another month. We feel secure when we receive our welfare checks, knowing we can pay rent. In the winter we rejoice over the HEAP (heating assistance) Program, knowing we will be warm during the cold weather. We are grateful for WIC (women, infants, and children): milk, formula, and juice for our young children. The medical card is treasured as if it were gold.

Our children can go to the doctor. Our children receive free lunches. Daycare is provided. We drink in help from all the agencies. We are grateful for the churches that provide food pantries. Our food stamps sometimes do not last until the end of the month.

Full of fear, we go off to college. Dreams of being "somebody" dance in our heads. A hope for a better life and the promise of a brighter future for our children gives us inner strength. We drive off in our "junkers," praying that we will not have car trouble today. We pack our lunches. We live one day at a time. Unless you have walked in our shoes—do not judge us.

How Do We Get Off Welfare?
Welfare + Help From Social Agencies + A College Education + Child Support + Some Help From Our Churches = A Job With Medical Benefits, Food On The Table, and Shelter.

Then we give back to our society. We grow. We transform. We share. We laugh. We cry. We change. We encourage other single moms who are NOT GENERATIONAL WELFARE.

Chapter Thirteen

Tools for Change

[This chapter contains visual aids and activities to help victims and batterers. Counselors, pastors, helpers, support group leaders, etc. may use these tools. The resource section in the back of the book also lists videos, books and workbooks which may be used to help God's broken families.]

The power for change for the batterer is the indwelling of the Holy Spirit. Pastors and helpers can introduce the Christian batterer to a relationship with the Holy Spirit. Believers experience a "rebirth" as the Holy Spirit communicates God's power through their spirit.

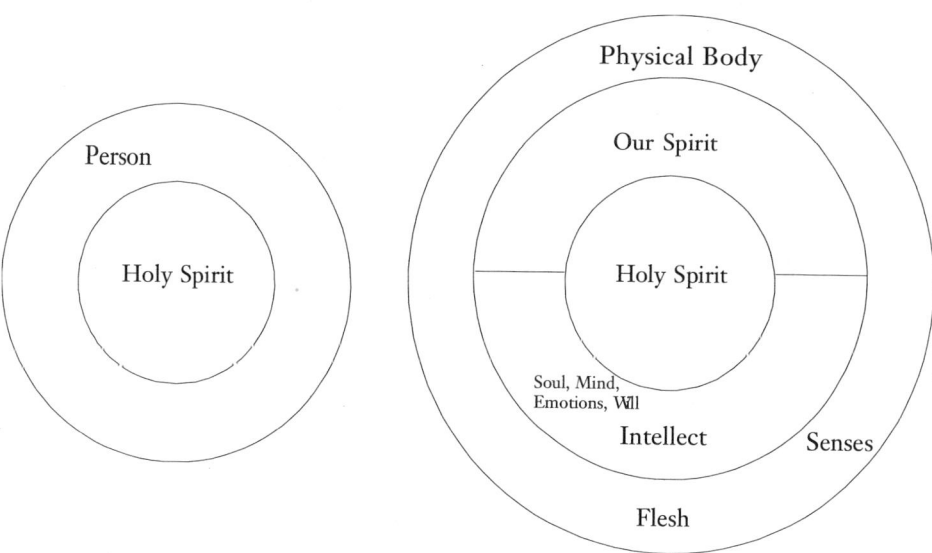

Watchman Nee in his book, *The Spiritual Man*, states:

> "Believers today very much lack knowledge of the existence and operation of the human spirit. Many are unaware that in addition to their minds, emotion and will they also have a spirit. Even when they have heard of the spirit, many Christians either consider their mind,

emotion, or will as the spirit or else plainly admit they know not where their spirit is. Such ignorance enormously affects cooperation with God, control over self, and war against Satan, the performance of which in all cases requires the operation of the spirit. It is imperative that believers recognize a spirit exists in them."[1]

John 14:16-17 states: "And I will ask the Father, and He will give you another Helper, that He may be with you forever; that is the Spirit of truth, whom the world cannot receive, because it does not behold Him or know Him, but you know Him because He abides with you, and will be in you."

How does a person acquire the Holy Spirit?

A person simply asks God for His Holy Spirit to dwell inside of him/her. (John 20:22) God will not fill a person with the Holy Spirit unless He owns the person. Accepting Jesus as your Savior is the prelude to the filling of the Holy Spirit. Luke 11:13 states, "If you then, though you are evil, know how to give good gifts to your children, how much more will your Father in Heaven give the Holy Spirit to those who ask him?" (NIV)

Watchman Nee also states:

"Man's spirit can be compared to an electric light bulb. When in contact with the Holy Spirit, it shines; but should it be disconnected, it plunges into darkness. The spirit of man is the lamp of the Lord. (Proverbs 20:27) God's aim is to fill the human spirit with light; yet the believer's spirit is sometimes darkened. Why is this? It is because it has lost contact with the Holy Spirit. To perceive whether or not one's spirit is connected with the Holy Spirit, one need only to notice if it is shining."[2]

Selected Scriptures in the New Testament about the Holy Spirit:

Matthew 1:20	Romans 15:13, 16	2 Timothy 1:14
Mark 3:29	1 Corinthians 3:16	Titus 3:5
Luke 1:35	1 Corinthians 6:19	Hebrews 2:4
John 14:20, 26	2 Corinthians 6:6	1 Peter 1:12
Acts 2:4	Galatians 5:16	2 Peter 1:21
Acts 10:44-45	Ephesians 4:30	1 John 5:7
Acts 11:16	1 Thessalonians 1:5	Jude 2
		Revelation 1:10

Tools for Change

When the Holy Spirit is at the center of our emotions, we will be in balance and experience the fruits of the spirit (Galatians 5:22). If Jesus is not at the center, we will be out of balance. Our core will be faulty. Battering men experience out-of-balance emotions. Their core is based on human power instead of Holy Spirit power. "Holy" is the key word. The Holy Spirit helps us to be holy and to act holy. Self at the core produces selfishness.

How do you know what is at the center/core of your life? Ask yourself this question: "What do I think about the most?" The deeds of the flesh are evident, which are: immorality, impurity, sensuality, idolatry, sorcery, enmities, strife, jealousy, outbursts of anger, disputes, dissensions, factions. (Galatians 5:19-20)

God Wants Us to Have a Balanced Life

God created us to be physical, emotional, and spiritual beings. Each area can grow out of balance in a Christian's life. Battering men do not experience a balanced life.

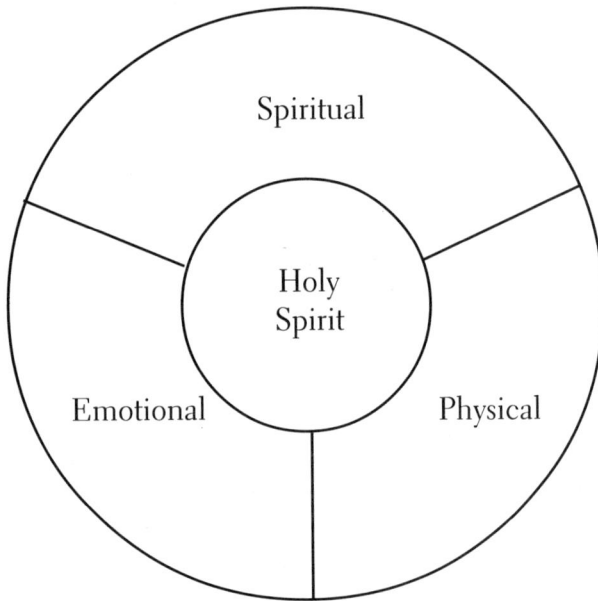

Anger Management Contract

I, _____, agree to change my violent behaviors.

I will read the contents of this manual and apply the practices to my life daily.

I will read and meditate on the scriptures about anger.

I will pray and ask the Holy Spirit to help me.

I will practice anger management methods.

I will attend a Christian support group for male batterers.

I promise NEVER again to physically assault my wife or children.

Signed by _____
Date _____

Witnessed by _____
Date _____

Anger Management Kit

Purpose: To educate battering men about the prelude to violent anger in order to prevent violent behaviors and assault.

PHYSICAL

Body cues:
increased blood pressure
red face
pressure in chest area
shaking
sweating
tensing of muscles
dizziness
posture change
facial expressions
clenched teeth
short breaths

EMOTIONAL

Body cues:
yelling
frustration
embarrassed
irritation
anger
fear
insecure/helpless
jealousy
suspicious
hysterical
anxious

COGNITIVE

Body cues:
irrational thoughts
jumbled thoughts
paranoid thoughts
confusion
blaming family
shaming family
mistrust
bad day at work
financial stress
thoughts of past abuse
life is unfair thoughts

SPIRITUAL

Body Cues:
disconnected from God
lack of praying
lack of reading Bible
lack of conviction
lack of conscience
angry with God
angry with your pastor
feels condemnation
blames God
shouts submission
misquotes scriptures

VERBAL

Body Cues:
voice tone elevates
name calling
hurtful remarks
"you" statements

BEHAVIORS

Body Cues:
slams fist
points finger
squeezes hands
towers over wife

PREVENTION METHODS
When you recognize the above behaviors, take immediate action:

PHYSICAL
leave area
take a walk
go to another room
allow wife to leave area
deep breathing exercises
jump in a cold shower
call member of support group

COGNITIVE
self-talk
identify irrational thoughts
change thinking pattern
remind yourself of jail
remind yourself of separation
look at her fears
apologize to family members

EMOTIONAL
identify emotions
put yourself in her shoes
feelings can't be trusted
consequences of emotions
put self in children's shoes

SPIRITUAL
ask Holy Spirit to help you
confess anger to God
kneel in prayer
call your pastor
call accountability partner

BEHAVIORS
go outside and play basketball
do any physical activity
release tension in nonviolent ways

Help the batterer to make his own list of alternative behaviors.

Battering men are like factories continually producing anger. The recipe for violent anger is to continually put in negative ingredients. Whatever ingredients you put into cake batter will determine the taste and texture of the cake. All of the batterer's emotions gravitate towards one emotion—ANGER. His goal is to obtain power and control over his wife and children.

Ingredients:	**Anger Factory**	Finished product:
fear		anger
insecurity		anger
mistrust		anger
resentment		anger
bitterness		anger
jealousy		anger
guilt		anger
anxiety		anger
selfishness and pride		anger
confusion		anger
sadness		anger
powerlessness		anger
rejection		anger
childhood abuse		anger
fear of abandonment		anger
unconfessed sin		anger
stress		anger
depression and apathy		anger
lies and deception		anger
blame and denial		anger
shame		anger
unsubmissive to God		anger
no self-esteem		anger
inaccurate view of God		anger
demoniac oppression		anger
wrong thinking/weak conscience		anger

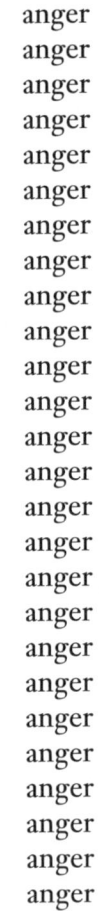

Violent crime and domestic abuse may be provoked by violent childhood punishment. This adult experiences the unresolved "frozen" childhood anger left over from the past. This internal anger is subconscious. He experiences the anger of a child in an adult body.

Thought-stopping map and behavior chain

- List ways to stop your negative thoughts before they turn into negative behaviors.
- List thoughts and behaviors that escalate into violence.
- List ways to stop your anger before it escalates into violent anger.
- List thoughts and behaviors that will prevent violence.

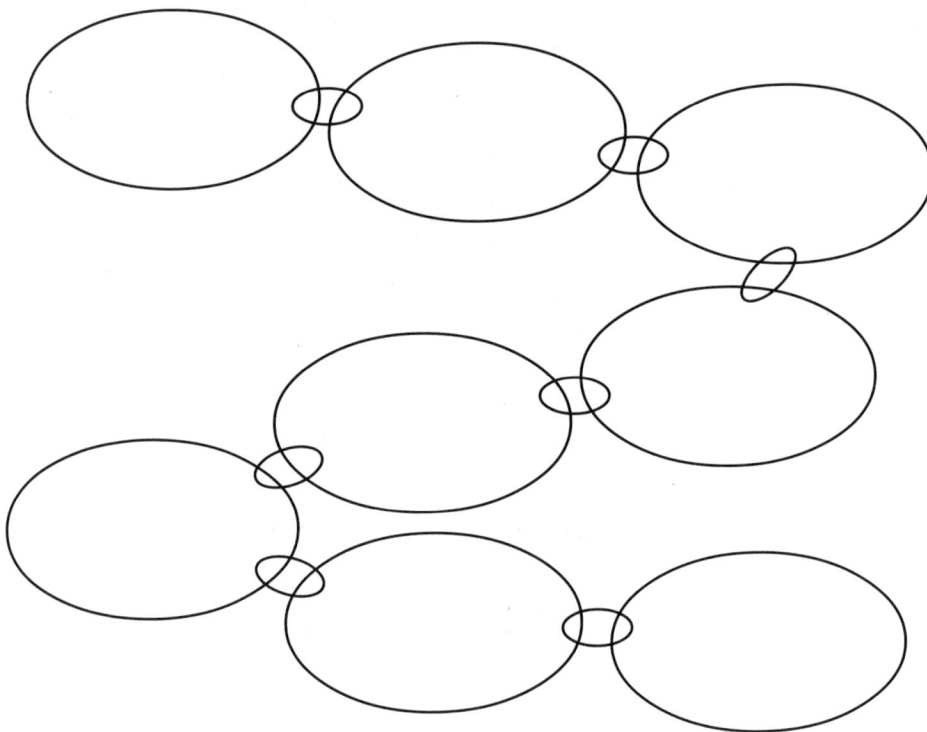

Mirror exercise

Purpose: 1) To generate discussion to find out the person's view of self and view of God.
2) To measure a person's self-image.

Tools: A mirror

Techniques: Hold up a mirror to the person and ask:

- What do you see?
- Describe the person in the mirror.

- What does God see?
- Describe how God sees you.
- How does your wife see you?
- How do your children see you?
- On a scale of one to ten, with ten being the highest, pick a number that describes how you like what you see.

Clergy, counselors, or helpers can read Bible verses that describe our value to God. If the person does not like what he sees:

- generate ways he can change
- explore low self-image
- explore view of self
- explore his/her view of God

Tools for therapy—the Genograph

A genograph is a visual tool used to trace the past history of violence in a family by looking at the previous generations. The purpose of the genograph for therapy with the batterer is:

1. To show the pattern of generational family violence and how it is repeated.
2. To show that family violence is a learned behavior and therefore can be unlearned.
3. To help the batterer understand how and why he became an abuser.
4. To display a visual graph to help with the learning process.
5. To show the batterer that his children will continue the cycle of abuse if he doesn't change.
6. To stimulate memories to explore emotions related to past events and experiences.
7. To show how family members relate to each other.
8. To explore family values, attitudes, rules, and personalities.
9. To look at family losses and problems.

The Book of Matthew opens with a family tree of Jesus' ancestors. Jesus' family tree hides nothing. God allowed every disgusting and secret deed of his people to be revealed in the Bible. God will not hide our sins. God will not allow us to hide our sins. The purpose of discussing Jesus' genograph is:

1. To show that Jesus came from a line of imperfect human beings.
2. To show that Jesus uses imperfect people who make mistakes, if they repent.
3. To show the forgiveness of God.
4. To show how continued sin produces spiritual death.
5. To show how the sins of the fathers are passed on to their children.

A genograph is not used for the purpose of excusing violent behavior. The purpose is to educate the batterer so he can begin the healing process. Education and knowledge are tools for understanding and changing our thoughts and behaviors.

- Jesus is from the lineage of King David.
- David committed adultery with Bathsheba.
- David had Bathsheba's husband murdered.
- David's daughter Tamar was raped by his son Amnon.
- David did not address the rape.
- David's son Absalom killed his brother Amnon because of the rape.
- Absalom tried to kill his father, David.
- Absalom was killed by David's army.
- David's son Solomon was an alcohol abuser who had sexual relations with 900 women.

King David and King Solomon repented of their sins, and God once again blessed them. But, both still suffered the consequences of sin.

Battering men need to know that God will forgive them and still use them for the Kingdom of Heaven. God still has a purpose for their lives. We are all sinners saved by grace.

Genograph directions

1. List husband and wife.

2. List their father and mother.

3. List paternal and maternal grandparents.

4. Use the following codes to label behaviors of each generation. Use different colors of ink for clarity.

CODES:

AA = alcoholism
A = problem with anger
AC = attended church
AD = adultery
B = read Bible together
BF = blended family
C = Christian/religious
CO = codependency
D = divorce
DD = deaths in family
DP = depression
DV = domestic violence
EA = economic abuse
EM = emotional abuse
FA = father abandoned family
HT = head trauma
J = extreme jealousy
MI = mental illness
MU = murder of a family member
NA = drugs
NR = narcissistic traits
PA = physical abuse
PAA = parental authority abuse
PL = pathological lying
PO = pornography use
PRA = prayed together
PRI = spent time in prison
SA = sexual abuse
SO = social abuse
VA = verbal abuse
SP = spiritual abuse

[Genograph chart on next page]

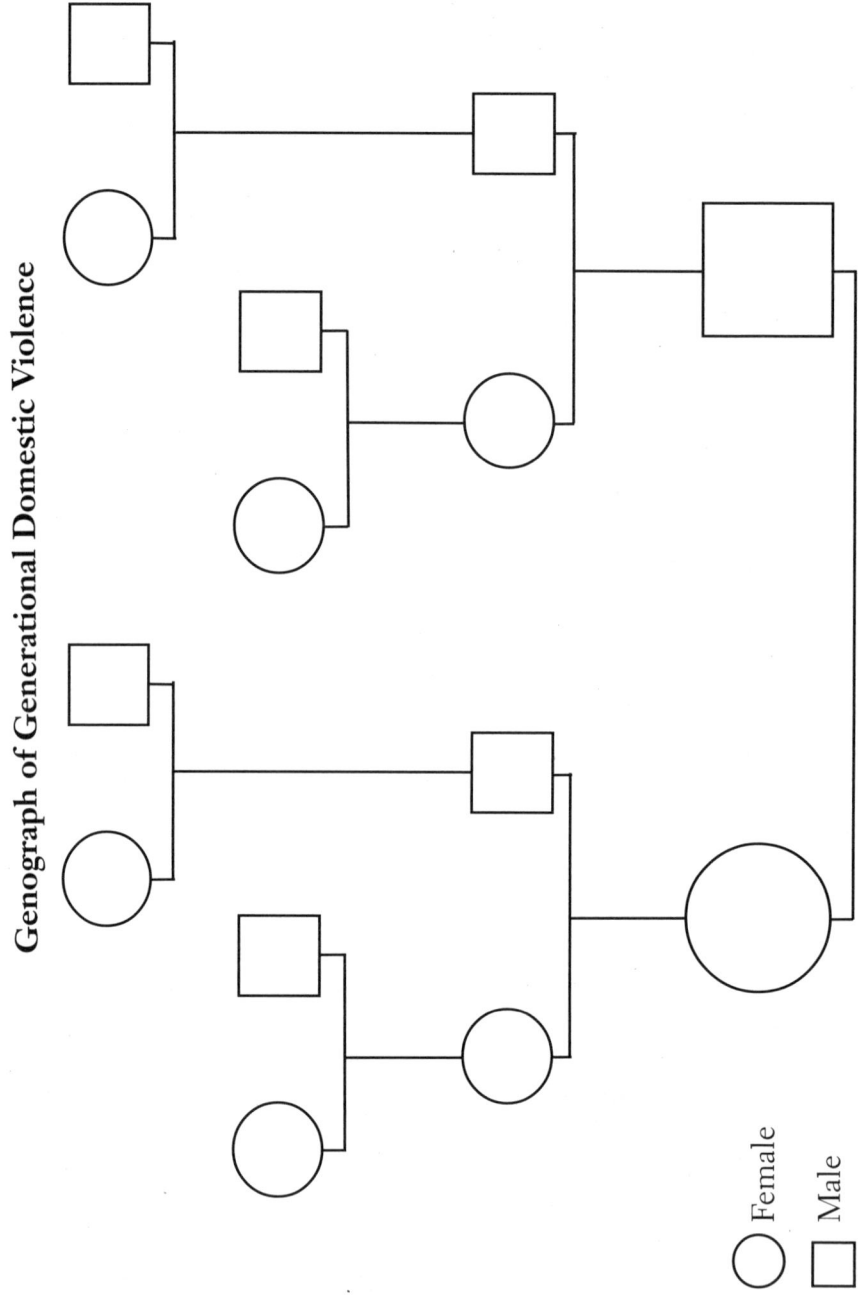

Scriptures for Renewing of the Mind

Changing Your Thinking and Controlling your Thoughts

Luke 24:45	Then He opened their **minds** to understand the scriptures.
Romans 7:25	So then, on the one hand I myself with my **mind** am serving the law of God.
Romans 8:27	And He who searches the hearts knows what the **mind** of the spirit is because He intercedes for the saints according to the will of God.
Romans 12:2	And do not be conformed to this world, but be transformed by the renewing of your **mind**.
Romans 12:16	Be of the same **mind** toward one another; do not be haughty in **mind**, but associate with the lowly. Do not be wise in your own estimation.
Romans 14:5	One man regards one day above another, another regards every day alike. Let each man be fully convinced in his own **mind**.
Romans 15:5	Now may the God who gives perseverance and encouragement grant you to be of the same **mind** with one another according to Christ Jesus.
1 Corin. 1:10	Now I exhort you brethren, by the name of our Lord Jesus Christ, that you all agree, and there be no divisions among you, but you be made complete in the same **mind** and in the same judgment.
1 Corin. 14:14	For if I pray in a tongue, my spirit prays, but my **mind** is unfruitful.
1 Corin. 14:15	What is the outcome then? I shall pray with the spirit with the **mind** also; I shall sing with the spirit and I shall sing with the **mind** also.

2 Corin. 5:13	For if we are beside ourselves, it is for God; if we are of sound **mind**, it is for you.
2 Corin. 10:5	We are taking every **thought** captive to the obedience of Christ.
2 Corin. 11:3	But I am afraid, lest as the serpent deceived Eve by his craftiness, your **minds** should be led astray from the simplicity and purity of devotion to Christ.
Ephes. 2:3	Among them we too all formerly lived in the lusts of our flesh, indulging the desires of the flesh and of the **mind**, and were by nature children of wrath, even as the rest.
Ephes. 4:23	And that you be renewed in the spirit of your **mind**.
Philip. 2:2	Make the joy complete by being of the same **mind**, maintaining the same love, united in spirit, intent on one purpose.
Philip. 3:19	Whose end is destruction, whose god is their appetite, and glory is in their shame, who set their **minds** on earthly things.
Philip. 4:7	And the peace of God, which surpasses all comprehension, shall guard your hearts and your **minds** in Christ Jesus.
Philip. 4:8	Finally, brethren, whatever is true, whatever is honorable, whatever is right, whatever is pure, whatever is lovely, whatever is of good repute, if there is any excellence and if anything worthy of praise, let your **mind** dwell on these things.
Colos. 1:21	And although you were formerly alienated and hostile in **mind**, engaged in evil deeds.
Colos. 2:18	Let no one keep defrauding you of your prize by delighting in self-abasement and the worship of angels, taking his stand on visions he has seen, inflated without cause by his fleshly **mind**.

Colos. 3:2	Set your **mind** on the things above, not on the things that are on earth.
Thessa. 1:3	Constantly bearing in **mind** your work of faith and labor of love and steadfastness of hope in our Lord Jesus Christ in the presence of our God and Father.
2 Tim. 3:8	And just as Jannes and Jambres opposed Moses, so these men also oppose the truth, men of depraved **mind**, rejected as regards the faith.
Titus 1:15	To the pure, all things are pure; but to those who are defiled and unbelieving, nothing is pure, but both their **mind** and their conscience are defiled.
James 1:7,8	For let not that man expect that he will receive anything from the Lord, being a double-**minded** man, unstable in all his ways.
James 4:8	Draw near to God and He will draw near to you. Cleanse your hands, you sinners; and purify your hearts, you double-**minded**.
1 Peter 1:13	Therefore, gird your **minds** for action, keep sober in spirit, fix your hope completely on the grace to be brought to you at the revelation of Jesus Christ.
Jude 1:19	These are the ones who cause divisions, worldly-**minded**, devoid of the spirit.

Self-talk and positive thinking exercises

Purpose: To develop a plan for right thinking and positive self-talk.

1. PAY ATTENTION TO YOUR INTERNAL DIALOGUE. ASK YOURSELF QUESTIONS:
   - What do I tell myself?
   - How can I change what I tell myself?
   - Is what I tell myself true or false?
   - Is there any evidence to support what I tell myself? Are there any facts?
   - Are my thoughts lies from Satan?
   - What purpose are my negative thoughts serving?
   - What purpose does my behavior serve?

2. LEARN THE FOLLOWING:
   - I talk to myself.
   - I listen to myself.
   - I take action on what I tell myself.

<u>Example of negative thinking and self-talk</u>:

Self-talk: *"My wife looks nice today. Why does she look so nice when she is just going to work? I bet she wants to look nice for the guy in her office."*

Listen: *"Yes, she wants to date the guy in her office."*
Action: *"I'm going to go see her at work and confront her about her boyfriend!"*

<u>Example of turning negative thinking into positive thinking by self-talk</u>:

Self-talk: *"My wife looks nice today. Why does she look so nice when she is just going to work? I bet she wants to look nice for the guy in her office."*

Listen: *"Wait a minute. Is what I am telling myself true or false? Are these thoughts lies from Satan? Are there any facts? She just colored her hair for the family reunion on Saturday. I do trust my wife. There is no proof of infidelity."*

Action: *"I will not go to her place of work and embarrass her. I know I have choices in every situation. I choose not to act on my negative thoughts. What purpose would it serve? We would get into a fight and then I might become angry or violent."*

3. ANALYZE YOUR THINKING AND BEHAVIOR PATTERNS:
   - identify problem thinking
   - identify problem listening
   - identify problem actions (behaviors)

4. KEEP A THINKING AND SELF-TALK JOURNAL:
   - keep a record of the negative thoughts and behaviors you changed
   - practice and write your daily progress

Appendix A

Directory of Resources

National Domestic Violence Hotline

1-800-799-SAFE (7233)

    The National Domestic Violence Hotline is staffed 24 hours a day by trained counselors who can provide crisis assistance and information about shelters, legal advocacy, health care centers, and counseling. There is also a toll-free number for the hearing-impaired, **1-800-787-3224 (TDD).**

RAINN Hotline: 1-800-656-HOPE

The Rape, Abuse, Incest National Network will automatically transfer you to the rape crisis center nearest you, anywhere in the nation. It can be used as a last resort if victims or helpers cannot find a domestic violence shelter.

National Resource Center on Domestic Violence: 1-800-537-2238

Call for a listing of domestic violence coalitions and catalogs.

National Domestic Violence Coalition's Main Office: (303) 839-1852

Call to order a *1997 National Directory of Domestic Violence Shelters*, which includes state maps at the beginning of each state section. Purchase price is $50, plus $7 for shipping and handling. Send your order to: The National Coalition Against Domestic Violence, P.O. Box 18749, Denver, CO, 80218.

Other resources include:
Resource manual: *Working with Women with Disabilities*
Resource manual: *Teen Dating*
General information packet: *Every Home a Safe Home*
Catalog: T-shirts, bumper stickers, posters, mugs, etc.

State Toll-Free Hotlines

Arkansas
1-800-332-4443
Florida
1-800-500-1119
Indiana
1-800-334-7233
LA County
1-800-978-3600
Michigan
1-800-996-6228
Montana
(24 hours) 1-800-655-7867
Nevada
1-800-992-5757
New Hampshire
1-800-852-3311
New Jersey
1-800-572-7233
New York
(English) 1-800-942-6906
New York
(Spanish) 1-800-942-6908
North Dakota
1-800-472-2911
Oklahoma
1-800-522-7233
Pennsylvania
1-800-642-3150
Texarkana area
1-800-876-4808
Vermont
1-800-228-7395
Virginia
1-800-838-8238
West Virginia
1-800-352-6513
Washington
1-800-562-6025
Wisconsin
1-800-333-7233
Wyoming
1-800-445-7233

Domestic Violence Directory for Ohio (1998)

These resources are presented as an example of the large number of shelters that are available in one state. Check your local listings for shelters in your area.

COUNTY	SHELTER	PHONE
Allen	Crossroads Crisis Center	419-228-4357
Ashland	The Domestic Violence Shelter, Inc.	800-931-7233
Ashtabula	Homesafe, Inc.	440-992-2727
Athens	My Sister's Place	800-443-3402
Auglaize	Auglaize County Crisis Center	419-738-5511
Belmont	Women's Tri-County Help Center	800-695-1639
Brown	YWCA House of Peace	513-753-7281
Butler	Dove House	513-863-7099
		800-543-1399
Carroll	Domestic Violence Project	330-452-6000
Champaign	Project Woman	800-634-9893
Clark	Project Woman	800-634-9893

County	Organization	Phone
Clermont	YWCA House of Peace	513-753-7281
Clinton	YWCA House of Peace	513-753-7281
Columbiana	SAVE	330-424-7774
Coshocton	Transitions	614-454-3213
Crawford	Turning Point	800-232-6505
Cuyahoga	Women Together	216-391-4357
	East Side Catholic Shelter	216-641-8989
	Templum House	216-631-2275
Darke	Shelter from Violence	937-548-2020
Defiance	Northwestern Ohio Crisis Line	419-782-1100
Delaware	CHOICES	740-224-4663
	Turning Point	800-232-6505
Erie	Genesis House	216-323-3400
	Safe Harbor	419-626-2200
Fairfield	The Lighthouse, Inc.	740-687-4423
Fayette	Project Woman	800-634-9893
Franklin	CHOICES	614-224-4663
	Point of Decision	800-923-7822
Fulton	YWCA Battered Women Shelter	419-241-7386
	Northwestern Ohio Crisis Line	419-782-1100
Galia	Serenity House	800-252-5554
Geauga	WomanSafe	216-564-9555
Greene	Greene County Domestic Violence Project	937-372-4552
Guernsey	Haven of Hope	740-432-3542
Hamilton	Alice Paul House	513-241-2757
Hancock	Open Arms	419-422-4766
Hardin	Crossroads Crisis Center	419-228-4357
Harrison	Women's Tri-County Help Center	800-695-1639
Henry	Northwestern Ohio Crisis Line	419-782-1100
Highland	Highland County Domestic Task Force	937-393-8118
Hocking	My Sister's Place	800-443-3402
Holmes	Every Woman's House	330-263-1020
Huron	The Domestic Violence Shelter, Inc.	800-931-7233
	Safe Harbor	419-626-2200
Jackson	Serenity House	800-252-5554
Jefferson	ALIVE	740-283-3444
Knox	New Directions	419-397-4357
Lake	Forbes House	216-357-1018
Lawrence	Lawrence County Domestic Violence Shelter	740-532-7111
Licking	New Beginnings	800-686-2760
Logan	Project Woman	800-634-9893
Lorain	Genesis House	216-323-3400
Lucas	YWCA Battered Women Shelter	419-241-7386
Madison	CHOICES	740-224-4663
	A Friend's House Crisis Hotline	740-852-8900
	Project Woman	800-634-9893

County	Organization	Phone
Mahoning	Sojourner House	330-747-4040
Marion	Turning Point	800-232-6505
Medina	Battered Women's Shelter	330-374-1111
Meigs	Serenity House	800-252-5554
Mercer	Family Crisis Network	419-586-1133
Miami	Family Abuse Shelter	937-339-6761
Monroe	Women's Tri-County Help Center	800-695-1639
Montgomery	YWCA Shelter & Housing Network	937-222-8946
Morgan	Transitions	740-454-3213
Morrow	Turning Point	800-232-6505
Muskingum	Transitions	740-454-3213
Noble	EVE	740-374-5819
Ottawa	YWCA Battered Women Shelter	419-241-7386
	Safe Harbor	419-626-2200
Paulding	Northwestern Ohio Crisis Line	419-782-1100
Perry	Transitions	740-454-3213
Pickaway	Haven House	740-447-9113
Pike	SAVSA	740-947-1611
Portage	Safer Futures	330-678-4357
Preble	Preble County Counseling Center and Domestic Violence Center	800-480-6201
Putnam	Crime Victims Services	419-523-1111
Richland	The Domestic Violence Shelter, Inc.	800-931-7233
Ross	Ross County Coalition Against Domestic Violence/Phoenix House (crisis line)	740-775-5396 / 740-773-4357
Sandusky	First Step	419-435-7300
Scioto	Southern Ohio Task Force	740-456-8217
Seneca	First Step	419-435-7300
Shelby	New Choices	937-498-7261
Stark	Alliance Area Domestic Violence Center	330-823-7223
	Domestic Violence Project	330-453-7233
Summit	Battered Women's Shelter	330-374-1111
Trumbull	Someplace Safe	330-393-1565
Tuscarawas	Harbor House	330-364-1374
Union	CHOICES	937-224-4663
	Turning Point	800-232-6505
Van Wert	Crisis Care Line	419-238-4357
Vinton	My Sister's Place	800-443-3402
Warren	Warren County Family Abuse Shelter	513-933-1107
Washington	EVE	740-374-5819
Wayne	Every Woman's House	330-263-1020
Williams	Northwestern Ohio Crisis Line	419-782-1100
Wood	First Step	419-435-7300
Wyandot	Turning Point	800-232-6505

Domestic Violence Coalitions in the United States

ALABAMA
Alabama Coalition Against Violence
Phone: (334) 832-4842
Fax: (334) 832-4803
P.O. Box 4762
Montgomery, AL 36101

ALASKA
Alaska Network on Domestic Violence and Sexual Assault
Phone: (907)586-3650
Fax: (907) 436-4493
130 Seward Street, Room 501
Juneau, AK 99801

ARIZONA
Arizona Coalition Against Domestic Violence
Phone: (602) 279-2900
or (800) 782-6400
Fax: (602) 279-2980
100 W. Camelback, #109
Phoenix, AZ 85013

ARKANSAS
Arkansas Coalition Against Violence to Women and Children
Phone: (501) 339-9486
Fax: (501) 371-0450
523 S. Louisiana, Suite 230
Little Rock, AR 72201

CALIFORNIA
California Alliance Against Domestic Violence
Phone: (209) 524-1888
Fax: (209) 524-2045
619 13th St., Suite-I
Modesto, CA 95354

SOUTHERN CALIFORNIA
Coalition Against Domestic Violence
Phone: (213) 655-6098
P.O. Box 5036
Santa Monica, CA 90405

COLORADO
Colorado Domestic Violence Coalition
P.O. Box 18902
Denver, CO 80218
Phone: (303) 573-9018
Fax: (303) 573-9023

CONNECTICUT
Connecticut Coalition Against Domestic Violence
Phone: (860) 524-5890
Fax: (860) 249-1408
135 Broad Street
Hartford, CT 06105

DELAWARE
Delaware Coalition Against Domestic Violence
Phone: (302) 658-5049
Fax: (302) 658-5049
P.O. Box 847
Wilmington, DE 19899

FLORIDA
Florida Coalition Against Domestic Violence
Phone: (904) 668-6862
Fax: (904) 668-0364
1535-C5 Killearn Center Blvd.
Tallahassee, FL 32308

GEORGIA
Georgia Coalition Against Domestic Violence
Phone: (770) 984-0085
Fax: (770) 984-0068
1827 Powers Ferry Road
Atlanta, GA 30339

HAWAII
Hawaii State Committee on Family Violence
Phone: (808) 486-5072
Fax: (808) 486-5169
98-939 Moanalua Road
Aiea, HI 96701-5012

IDAHO
Idaho Coalition Against Sexual and Domestic Violence
Phone: (208)384-0419
Fax: (208)384-0419
200 North 4th Street, Suite 10-K
Boise, ID 83702

ILLINOIS
Illinois Coalition Against Domestic Violence
Phone: (217) 789-2830
Fax: (217) 789-1939
730 E. Vine St., Suite 109
Springfield, IL 62703

INDIANA
Indiana Coalition Against Domestic Violence, Inc.
Phone: (317) 543-3908
Fax: (317) 568-4045
2511 E. 46th St., Suite N-3
Indianapolis, IN 46205

IOWA
Iowa Coalition Against Domestic Violence
Phone: (515) 244-8028
Fax: (515) 244-7417
1540 High St., Suite 100
Des Moines, IA 50309-3123

KANSAS
Kansas Coalition Against Sexual and Domestic Violence
Phone: (913) 232-9784
Fax: (913) 232-9937
820 SE Quincy, Suite 416
Topeka, KS 66612

KENTUCKY
Kentucky Domestic Violence Association
Phone: (502) 875-4132
Fax: (502) 875-4268
P.O. Box 356
Frankfort, KY 40602

LOUISIANA
Louisiana Coalition Against Domestic Violence
Phone: (504) 542-4446
Fax: (504) 542-7661
P.O. Box 3053
Hammond, LA 70404-3053

MAINE
Maine Coalition for Family Crisis Services
Phone: (207) 941-1194
Fax: (207) 941-1194
128 Main St.
Bangor, ME 04402

MARYLAND
Maryland Network Against Domestic Violence
Phone: (301) 942-0900
Fax: (301) 929-2589
11501 Georgia Avenue, Suite 403
Silver Spring, MD 20902

MASSACHUSETTS
Massachusetts Coalition of Battered Women Services
Phone: (617) 248-0922
Fax: (617) 248-0902
210 Commercial St., 3rd Fl.
Boston, MA 02109

MICHIGAN
Michigan Coalition Against Domestic Violence
Phone: (517) 484-2924
Fax: (517) 372-0024
P.O. Box 16009
Lansing, MI 48901

MINNESOTA
Minnesota Coalition for Battered Women
Phone: (612) 646-6177
Fax: (612) 646-1527
1619 Dayton Avenue, Suite 303
St. Paul, MN 55104

Appendix

MISSISSIPPI
Mississippi Coalition Against Domestic Violence
Phone: (601) 981-9196
Fax: (601) 982-7372
P.O. Box 4703
Jackson, MS 39296-4703

MISSOURI
Missouri Coalition Against Domestic Violence
Phone: (314) 634-4161
Fax: (314) 636-3728
331 Madison Street
Jefferson City, MO 65101

MONTANA
Montana Coalition Against Domestic Violence
Phone: (406) 256-6334
Fax: (406) 256-6334
1236 North 28th Street
Billings, MT 59101

NEBRASKA
Nebraska Domestic Violence and Sexual Assault Coalition
Phone: (402) 476-6256
Fax: (402) 477-0837
315 South 9th, #18
Lincoln, NE 68508

NEVADA
Nevada Network Against Domestic Violence
Phone: (702) 358-1171
Fax: (702) 358-0546
2100 Capurro Way, Suite E
Sparks, NV 89413

NEW HAMPSHIRE
New Hampshire Coalition Against Domestic and Sexual Violence
Phone: (603) 224-8893
Fax: (603) 228-6096
P.O. Box 353
Concord, NH 03302-0353

NEW JERSEY
New Jersey Coalition for Battered Women
Phone: (603) 584-8107
Fax: (609) 584-9750
620 Whitehouse/Hamilton Sq. Rd.
Trenton, NJ 08690

NEW MEXICO
New Mexico State Coalition Against Domestic Violence
Phone: (505) 246-9240
Fax: (505) 246-9434
P.O. Box 25363
Albuquerque, NM 87125

NEW YORK
New York State Coalition Against Domestic Violence
Phone: (518) 432-4864
Fax: (518) 432-4864
79 Central Ave.
Albany, NY 12206

NORTH CAROLINA
North Carolina Coalition Against Domestic Violence
Phone: (919) 956-9124
Fax: (919) 682-1449
P.O. Box 51875
Durham, NC 27717

NORTH DAKOTA
North Dakota Council on Abused Women's Services
Phone: (701) 255-6240
Fax: (701) 255-1904
418 East Rosser Avenue, Suite 320
Bismarck, ND 58501

OHIO
Ohio Domestic Violence Network
Phone: (614) 784-0023
Fax: (614) 784-0033
4041 North High Street, #101
Columbus, OH 43214

Action Ohio Coalition For Battered Women
Phone: (614) 221-1255
20 S. Front Street
Columbus, OH 43215

OKLAHOMA
Oklahoma Coalition Against Domestic Violence and Sexual Assault
Phone: (405) 557-1210
Fax: (405) 557-1296
2200 N. Classen Blvd., Suite 610
Oklahoma City, OK 73106

OREGON
Oregon Coalition Against Domestic and Sexual Violence
Phone: (503) 223-7411
Fax: (503) 223-7490
520 NW Davis, Suite 310
Portland, OR 97209

PENNSYLVANIA
Pennsylvania Coalition Against Domestic Violence
Phone: (717) 545-6400
Fax: (401) 545-9456
6400 Flank Drive, Suite 1300
Harrisburg, PA 17112

RHODE ISLAND
Rhode Island Coalition Against Domestic Violence
Phone: (401) 467-9940
Fax: (401) 467-9943
422 Post Road, Suite 104
Warwick, RI 02888

SOUTH CAROLINA
South Carolina Coalition Against Domestic Violence and Sexual Assault
Phone: (803) 254-3699
Fax: (803) 583-9611
P.O. Box 7776
Columbia, SC 29202-7776

SOUTH DAKOTA
South Dakota Coalition Against Domestic Violence and Sexual Assault
Phone: (605) 945-0869
Fax: (605) 945-0870
P.O. Box 141
Pierre, SD 57501

TENNESSEE
Tennessee Task Force Against Domestic Violence
Phone: (615) 386-9406
Fax: (615) 383-2967
P.O. Box 120972
Nashville, TN 37212

TEXAS
Texas Council on Family Violence
Phone: (512) 794-1133
Fax: (512) 794-1199
8701 N. Mopac Expressway, Suite 450
Austin, TX 78759-8364

UTAH
Domestic Violence Advisory Council
Phone: (801) 538-4100
Fax: (801) 538-3993
120 North, 200 West, Suite 225
Salt Lake City, UT 84145

VERMONT
Vermont Network Against Domestic Violence and Sexual Assault
Phone: (802) 223-1302
Fax: (802) 223-3715
P.O. Box 405
Montpelier, VT 05601

VIRGINIA
Virginians Against Domestic Violence
Phone: (804) 221-0990
Fax: (804) 229-1553
2850 Sandy Bay Rd., Suite 101
Williamsburg, VA 23185

WASHINGTON
Washington State Coalition Against Domestic Violence
Phone: (360) 352-4029
Fax: (360) 352-4078
2101 4th Avenue E., Suite 103
Olympia, WA 98506

WASHINGTON, D.C.
DC Coalition Against Domestic Violence
Phone: (202) 783-5332
Fax: (202) 387-5684
513 U Street NW
Washington, DC 20001

WEST VIRGINIA
West Virginia Coalition Against Domestic Violence
Phone: (304) 765-2250
Fax: (304) 765-5071
P.O. Box 85
181 B Main Street
Sutton, WV 26601-0085

WISCONSIN
Wisconsin Coalition Against Domestic Violence
Phone: (608) 255-0539
Fax: (608) 255-3560
1400 East Washington Ave., #232
Madison, WI 53703

WYOMING
Wyoming Coalition Against Domestic Violence and Sexual Assault
Phone: (307) 266-4334
Fax: (307) 235-4796
341 E."E" Street, Suite 135A
Casper, WY 82601

Domestic violence coalitions are not shelters. They are national non-profit organizations focusing on education, prevention, child welfare, public policy reform, and referrals. Coalitions will refer women to domestic violence shelters in their counties.

National Religious Organizations Against Domestic Violence

Center for the Prevention of Domestic Violence and Sexual Assault
An inter-religious, educational ministry
Executive Director, Rev. Dr. Marie Fortune
936 North 34th St., Suite 200
Seattle, Washington 98103   (206) 634-1903   Fax: (206) 634-0115
Video and Study Guide: "Broken Vows,"—Religious Perspectives on DV, Parts I and II, available for rent ($50) or purchase ($139).

Catholic Social Services
Cecilia Held
P.O. Box 23825
Green Bay, WI 54305-3825
(414) 437-7531

Commission For Women
Evangelical Lutheran Church in America
8765 West Higgins Rd., Chicago, Illinois 60631
(773) 380-2860 or (312) 380-2860 or 1-800-638-3522, ext.2858
Fax: (312) 380-2997

Publishes: *If You Have Been Sexually Abused or Harassed*. A guide to getting effective help in the ECLA and a bibliography on sexual abuse and sexual harassment.

Committee on the Status of Women
The Episcopal Church Center
815 Second Avenue, New York, NY 10017-4594
(800) 334-7626
Video: "Confronting Sexism and Violence," available free of charge.

Committee on Women in Society and in the Church
National Conference of Catholic Bishops
Video: "When you Preach...Remember Me." Call 1-800-235-8722
Video No: 680-8 (12 minutes)
Pamphlet: *When I Call For Help*. A pastoral response to domestic violence against women. Publication No. 547-X

The Family Violence Project of Jewish Family Service
6851 Lennox Ave.
Van Nuys, CA 91405
(818) 908-5007

The Safer Society Program
P.O. Box 340
Brandon, VT 05733
(802) 247-3132 or the referral line (802) 247-5141
A national project of the New York State Council of Churches which maintains a national listing of agencies and treatment programs for young and adult violent offenders and sexual-abuse victims and offenders.

Women's Ministry Unit (WMU)
The Societal Violence Initiative Team
The Presbyterian Center
100 Witherspoon St., Room 3066B
Louisville, Kentucky 40202-1396
(502) 569-5811 Fax: (502) 569-8034
Publishes or distributes: *Myths and Facts About Rape and Battering; Family Violence: A Religious Issue*; and *The Doorway to Response* (on helping battered women). Resource Packet: *Confronting Violence Against Women, The Churches Calling*, available from the Presbyterian Distribution Service by calling 1-800-542-2612. Price: $6.00 per packet plus shipping and handling, refer to #72700 96002.

National Organizations Against Domestic Violence

Family Violence Prevention Fund
383 Rhode Island Street, Suite 304
San Francisco, CA 94103-5133
Phone: (415) 252-8900
Fax: (415) 252-8991
E-mail: fund@igc.apc.org

National Coalition Against Domestic Violence Policy Office
P.O. Box 34103
Washington, DC 20043-4103
Phone: (703) 765-339
Fax: (202) 628-4899

National Coalition Against Domestic Violence
P.O. Box 18749
Denver, CO 80218
Phone: (303) 839-1852
Fax: (303) 831-9251

National Battered Woman's Law Project
275 7th Avenue, Suite 1206
New York, NY 10001
Phone: (212) 741-9480
Fax: (212) 741-6438

National Resource Center On DV
Pennsylvania Coalition Against Domestic Violence
6400 Flank Drive, Suite 1300
Harrisburg, PA 17112
Phone: (800) 537-2238
Fax: (717) 545-9546

Battered Woman's Justice Project
Minnesota Program Development, Inc.
4032 Chicago Avenue South
Minneapolis, MN 55407
TOLL-FREE: 800-903-011, Ext.1
Phone: (612) 824-8768
Fax: (612) 824-8965

Resource Center on Child Custody and Child Protection
NCJFCJ
P.O. Box 8970
Reno, NV 89507
Phone: (800) 527-3223
Fax: (702) 784-6160

Battered Woman's Justice Project
c/o National Clearinghouse for the Defense of Battered Women
125 South 9th Street, Suite 302
Philadelphia, PA[[missing zip]]
TOLL-FREE: 800-903-0111, Ext. 3
Phone: (215) 351-0111
Fax: (215) 351-0779

National Clearinghouse on Marital and Date Rape
2325 Oak Street
Berkeley, CA 94708
Phone: (510) 524-1582

National Network to End Domestic Violence—Administrative Office
c/o Texas Council on Family Violence
8701 North Mopac Expressway, Suite 450
Austin, TX 78759
Phone: (512) 794-1133
Fax: (512) 794-1199

Battered Woman's Justice Project
c/o PCADV—Legal Office
524 McKnight Street
Reading, PA 19601
Phone: (610) 373-5697
Fax: (610) 373-6403

National Network to end Domestic Violence
701 Pennsylvania Avenue, NW, Suite 900
Washington, DC 20004

In Canada

National Clearinghouse on Family Violence
1-800-267-1291

Education Wife Assault
427 Bloor Street, West
Toronto, Ontario, Canada M5S 1X7
(416) 968-3422

Information About Treatment Programs and Resources for Male Batterers

Batterers Intervention Program
1276 W. 3rd St.
Cleveland, OH
(216) 443-5620

Learning to Live Without Violence by
Rev. Daniel J. Sonkin and Michael Durphy
San Franciso: Volcano Press, 1989
Manual for male batterers and counselors

Battering: An AMEND Manual for Helpers
(1984) by Wayne Ewing, Michael Lindsey
and Jan Pamerantz. Available from AMEND
P.O. Box 61281, Denver, CO 80206

Batterer's Anonymous (BA)
8485 Tamarind, Suite D
Fontana, CA 92335
(714) 355-1100

Men Stopping Violence
1020 DeKalb Ave., #25
Atlanta, Georgia 30307
(404) 688-1376

Emerge: A Men's Counseling Service
on Domestic Violence
18 Hurley St., Suite 23
Cambridge, MA 02141
(617) 422-1550

Domestic Violence Abuse Project, 1993
Men's Treatment Program Manual
Minneapolis, MN: DAP (612) 874-7063

MOVE (Men Overcoming Violence)
(415) 777-4496

NO ABUSE, Inc.
Orlando, Fl.
(407) 895-7151

Men Ending Domestic Violence
Illinois Center #3, Executive Woods
Belleville, IL 62221
1-800-782-1008 or (618) 235-5656

Pence, Ellen and Paymar, Michael
Duluth, MN, Intervention Project, 1993
New York, NY: Springer Publishing Co.

Court Mandated Treatment for Batterers
(1981) by Anne L. Ganley. Available from
the Center for Women's Policy Studies,
2000 P St. NW, Suite 508, Washington,
DC 20036

Please call your community Christian Counseling Centers, Christian Psychiatric Hospital, or local clergy, rabbis, or priests to find a Christian support/treatment/education group for male batterers in your area.

Please call your local domestic violence shelter/coalition or mental health agencies to find a secular support/treatment/education group for male batterers in your area.

Treatment Programs: Male Support Groups

Non-Religious
Batterers Anonymous
The goal is to stop spouse abuse through peer support and problem solving methods. Confrontation by peers is encouraged. Usually court-ordered by a judge.

Therapy:
- cognitive behavioral treatment
- communication training
- attitudes towards women challenged
- expectations of women explored
- anger management
- relaxation techniques
- physical exercise
- conflict resolution

Christian
Individual Groups

The goal is to stop spouse abuse through peer support and by Christian principles. Confrontation by Christian peers is encouraged. Family restoration is a priority if possible.

Treatment:
- confession and repentance
- renewing of mind by scriptures
- anger management
- root causes of violence
- prayer and accountability
- use Bible for manual and Christian workbooks
- use Christian resources
- Biblical way to treat wife; the truth about submission
- stress management and exercise
- marital counseling
- family counseling

Both non-religious and Christian batterers need assesment for the following:
- severity of injury to wife/partner
- use of weapon
- alcohol and/or drugs
- prior criminal record
- court ordered counseling
- reported for child abuse
- low reading level
- learning disability
- job skills
- mental illness
- head trauma
- loss of community status and reputation
- loss of position in the church

Motivators for change:
- police intervention and jail time
- having a felony record
- temporary and/or permanent separation

Christian Counseling Resources

Christian Comprehensive Care Corporation
4015 Executive Park Drive, Suite 305
Cincinnati, Ohio 45241
1-800-334-8973
(513) 769-4600

Minirith-Meier Clinic
2100 North Collins Boulevard
Richardson, Texas 75080
1-800-232-9462
1-800-229-4769

New Hope Christian Counseling Center
Inpatient/Outpatient Hospital Treatment
1208 Sixth Ave.
Huntington, WV 25719-1875
1-800-992-9189
(304) 526-9189

Rapha
8876 Gulf Freeway, Suite 130
Houston, Texas 77017
1-800-227-2657

The Christian Association of Psychological Studies
(membership: Christian psychologists, counselors, and social workers)
To request a directory of Christian mental health professionals in the United States and Canada, write:
>CAPS
>P.O. Box 628
>Blue Jay, CA 92317
>(714) 337-5117

National Religious AIDS Organizations and Hotlines

AIDS Advocacy in African American
Churches Project
611 Pennsylvania Ave. SE. 359
Washington, DC 20003
Phone: (202) 546-8587
Fax: (202) 546-8867

AIDS Ministry Network,
Christian Church
P.O. Box 4188,
East Lansing, MI 48826
Phone: (517) 355-9324
Fax: (517) 432-2662

AIDS National Interfaith Network
110 Maryland Ave. NE, Ste. 504
Washington, DC 20002
Phone: (202) 546-0807
Fax: (800) 288-9619

Brethren Mennonite AIDS Hotline
44 N. Queen St.
Lancaster, PA 17503
Phone: (717) 394-3380

Christian AIDS Services Alliance
P.O. Box 3612
San Rafael, CA 94912-3612
Phone: (410) 268-3442

The Congress of National
Black Churches
1225 Eye St. NW, Ste. 750
Washington, DC 20005-3914
Phone: (202) 371-1091

Lutheran AIDS Network
Holy Cross Church
1165 Seville Dr.
Pacifica, CA 94044
Phone: (415) 359-2710

National Catholic AIDS Network
P.O. Box 422984
San Francisco, CA 94142-2984
Phone: (707) 874-3031
Fax: (707) 874-1433

National Episcopal AIDS Coalition
2025 Pennsylvania Ave. NW,
Suite 508
Washington, DC 20006-1813
Phone: (202) 628-6628

Presbyterian AIDS Network
3060A Presbyterian Ctr.
100 Witherspoon St.
Louisville, KY 40202-1396
Phone: (502)569-5794

Seventh-Day Adventist
Kinship International
P.O. Box 7320,
Laguna Niguel, CA 92607
Phone: (714)248-1299

Southern Baptist Convention
Christian Life Commission
901 Commerce, Ste. 550
Nashville, TN 37203
Phone: (615) 244-2495

Union of American Hebrew
Congregations
Central Conference of American
Rabbis Joint Committee on AIDS
75 2nd Ave., Ste. 550
Needham Heights, MA 02194
Phone: (617)449-0404
Fax: (617)449-0419

United Church AIDS/HIV Network
700 Prospect Ave.
Cleveland, OH 44115
Phone: (216)736-3270
Fax: (216)736-3263

United Methodist HIV/AIDS
Ministries Network
475 Riverside Drive, Room 350
New York, NY 10115
Phone: (212)870-3909
Fax: (212)749-2641

Unitarian Universalist Association AIDS
Network
25 Beacon St.
Boston, MA 02108-2800
Phone: (617)742-2100
Fax: (617) 523-4123

State Child Support Enforcement Offices

State	Phone	State	Phone
Alabama	(205) 242-9300	Montana	(406) 444-4614
Alaska	(907) 276-3441	Nebraska	(402) 471-9125
Arizona	(602) 252-0236	Nevada	(702) 687-4744
Arkansas	(501) 682-8398	New Hampshire	(603) 271-4426
California	(916) 654-1556	New Jersey	(609) 588-2361
Colorado	(303) 866-5994	New Mexico	(505) 827-7200
Connecticut	(203) 566-3053	New York	(518) 474-9081
Delaware	(302) 577-4863	North Carolina	(919) 571-4120
DC	(202) 724-8800	North Dakota	(701) 224-3582
Florida	(904) 488-9900	Ohio	(614) 752-6561
Georgia	(404) 657-3851	Oklahoma	(405) 424-5871
Guam	(671) 475-3360	Oregon	(503) 986-2417
Hawaii	(808) 587-3700	Pennsylvania	(717) 787-3672
Idaho	(208) 334-5710	Puerto Rico	(809) 722-4731
Illinois	(217) 782-8768	Rhode Island	(401) 277-2409
Indiana	(317) 232-4894	South Carolina	(803) 737-5870
Iowa	(515) 281-5580	South Dakota	(605) 773-3641
Kansas	(913) 296-3237	Tennessee	(615) 741-1820
Kentucky	(502) 564-2285	Texas	(512) 463-2181
Louisiana	(504) 342-4780	Utah	(801) 538-4400
Maine	(207) 287-2886	Vermont	(802) 241-2319
Maryland	(410) 333-3979	Virgin Islands	(809) 774-5666
Massachusetts	(617) 727-4200	Virginia	(804) 692-2458
Michigan	(517) 373-7570	Washington	(206) 586-3162
Minnesota	(612) 296-2542	West Virginia	(304) 558-3780
Mississippi	(601) 359-4500	Wisconsin	(608) 266-9909
Missouri	(314) 751-4301	Wyoming	(307) 777-6948

Call the child support agency in your county for more information. Telephone numbers can be found in your local phone book.

National Pregnancy Help Resources

Heartbeat International
(614) 239-9433
Business Office:
1213 ½ South James Road
Columbus, Ohio 43227-1801

Heartbeat is a worldwide association of life-affirming pregnancy centers founded to assist persons involved in problem pregnancies and related distress. An annual directory of pregnancy centers throughout the world is available.

America's Crisis Pregnancy Helpline
1-800-672-2296
Bethany Christian Services
1-800-238-4269
Birthright Hotline
1-800-550-4900
CareNet
1-800-395-4357
Catholic Charities Crisis Pregnancy Hotline
1-800-CARE-002
Liberty Godparent Ministries
1-800-542-4453
Love Life Maternity Home
1-800-634-4890
National Life Center
1-800-848-5683
Nurturing Network
1-800-866-4666
Project Rachel Post-Abortion Help
1-800-593-2273

For a list of crisis pregnancy centers by state and county, see the Internet URL at http://www.toolcity.net/~pfl/women.html#national

National Crisis Hotlines for Teenagers

Alcohol & Drug Helpline
1-800-821-4357

Child Abuse Hotline
1-800-422-4453

Child Find of America
1-800-426-5678

Child Quest International
1-800-248-8020

Christian AIDS Services Alliance
1-410-268-3442

Cocaine Hotline
1-800-252-2463

Crisis Intervention for Adolescent Referral Service
1-800-621-3860

HIV & AIDS Information
1-800-342-2437

Missing Children's Network
1-800-235-3535

Runaway Hotline
1-800-392-3352

Runaway Switchboard
1-800-621-4000

Street Survival Project
1-800-942-8382

Toughlove, Inc
1-215-348-7090

United Church AIDS & HIV Network
1-216-736-3270

Youth Crisis Line
1-800-448-4663

Appendix B

Resources

Religious Resources

Domestic Violence:

Adams, Carol. *Woman Battering:* Creative Pastoral Care and Counseling Series. Mountlake Terrace, WA: Augsburg/Fortress Press, 1994.

Adams, Carol and Fortune, Marie, editors. *Violence Against Women and Children.* New York, NY: Continuum Publishing Co., 1995.

Alsdurf, James and Phyllis. *Battered Into Submission.* Downers Grove, Illinois: InterVarsity Press, 1989.

Brown, Joanne Carlson and Bohn, Carole, editors. *Christianity, Patriarchy, and Abuse.* Cleveland, Ohio: Pilgrim Press, 1989.

Busssert, Joy. *Battered Women: From a Theology of Suffering to an Ethic of Empowerment.* New York: Division for Mission in North America, Lutheran Church in America, 1986.

Clarke, Rita-Lou. *Pastoral Care of Battered Women.* Philadelphia: Westminster Press, 1986.

Cooper-White, Pamela. *The Cry of Tamar: Violence Against Women and the Church's Response.* Minneapolis: Fortress Press, 1995.

Fairless, Caroline. "*What Does Love Require? A Family Violence Manual for the Church Community.*" M. Div. Honors Thesis, Church Divinity School of the Pacific, Berkeley, CA, 1989.

Fortune, Marie, Rev. *Keeping the Faith: Questions and Answers for the Abused Woman.* New York, NY: Harper Collins Publishers, 1987.

Fortune, Marie, Rev. *Violence in the Family: A Workshop Curriculum for Clergy and Other Helpers.* Cleveland, Ohio: The Pilgrim Press, 1991.

Gray-Reneberg, Jeri. *Domestic Violence: A Public Health Education and Resource Guide.* Lincoln: Lincoln-Lancaster County Health Department, 1996.

Horton, Anne, and Williamson, Judith. *When Praying Isn't Enough.* Lexington, Mass: Lexington Books, 1988.

Jones, Ann, and Schechter, S. *When Love Goes Wrong: What to do When You Can't Do Anything Right.* New York, NY: Harper Collins Publishers, Inc., 1992.

MacHaffie, Barbara J. *Her Story: Women in Christian Tradition.* Philadelphia: Fortress Press, 1986.

Martin, Del, *Battered Wives.* rev.ed. San Francisco, CA: Volcano Press, 1981.

Poling, James. *The Abuse of Power: A Theological Problem.* Nashville: Abingdon Press, 1991.

Rinck, Margaret, J. *Christian Men Who Hate Women.* Grand Rapids, Michigan: Zondervan Publishing House, 1990.

Russ, I., Weber, S., and Ledley et al. *A Jewish Response to Domestic Violence.* Panorama City, CA: The Shalom Bayit Committee, 6851 Lennox Ave., 1993.

Savina, Lydia. *Help For the Battered Woman.* South Plainfield, New Jersey: Bridge Publishing, 1987.

Spitzer, Julie, Rabbi. *When Love is Not Enough: Spousal Abuse in Rabbinic and Contemporary Judaism.* New York, NY: National Federal of Temple Sisterhoods, 1991.

Strom, Kay Marshall. *In the Name of Submission.* Portland, Oregon: Multnomah Press, 1986.

Trible, Phyllis. *Texts of Terror.* Philadelphia: Fortress Press, 1984.

White, Evelyn C. *Chain Chain Change: For Black Women Dealing with Physical and Emotional Abuse.* Seattle: Seal Press, 1985.

Church History and Violence Against Women:

Davidson, Terry. "Wifebeating: A Recurring Phenomenon throughout History, in *Battered Women: A Psychosociological Study of Domestic Violence*, ed. Maria Roy. New York, NY: Van Nostrand Reinhold, 1977, pp. 2-23.

Davis-Gould, Elizabeth. *The First Sex.* New York, NY: Putnam, 1971.

O'Faolain, Julia and Martines, Lauro, eds. *Not in God's Image: A History of Women in Europe from the Greeks to the Nineteenth Century.* New York, NY: Harper & Row, 1973.

The Significance of Women:

Johnson, Lela. *The Beautiful Side of Submission.* North Brunswick, NJ: Bridge-Logo, 1996.

Price, Eugenia. *God Speaks To Women Today.* Grand Rapids, Michigan: Zondervan Publishing House, 1964.

Marriage:

Frank, Jan and Don. *When Victims Marry.* San Bernardino, CA: Here's Life Publisher, 1990.

Swindoll, Charles. *Strike The Original Match.* Portland, OR: Multnomah Press, 1980.

Healing:

Frankl, Victor. *Man's Search For Meaning.* New York, NY: Simon & Schuster, Inc., Copyright © 1984.

Sanford, John and Paula. *Transformation of the Inner Man.* South Plainfield, NJ: Bride Publishing, 1982.

Seamands, David. *Healing of Memories.* Wheaton, Illinois: Victor Books, 1985.

Sexual Child Abuse:

Frank, Jan and Don. *A Door of Hope.* San Bernadino, CA: Here's Life Publisher, 1987.

Littauer, Fred. *Promise of Restoration.* San Bernadino, CA: Here's Life Publisher, 1990.

Reporting Child Abuse:

Fortune, Maria. "Reporting Child Abuse: An Ethical Mandate for Ministry" in *Abuse and Religion*, eds. Anne Horton and Judity Williamson, Lexington, Mass: Lexington Books, 1988.

View of God as Father:

Trent, John and Smalley, Gary. *The Blessing.* New York, New York: Pocketbooks, 1986.

Prayer:

Duewel, Wesley L. *Mighty Prevailing Prayer.* Grand Rapids, Michigan: Zondervan Publishing House, 1990.

Nee, Watchman. *The Spiritual Man.* New York, NY: Christian Fellowship Publishers, 1968.

Bible Study:
Halley, Henry, H. *Halley's Bible Handbook*. Grand Rapids, Michigan: Zondervan Publishing House, Twenty-fourth Edition, Copyright © 1996.

Newsome, Carol and Ringe, Sharon. *The Women's Bible Commentary*. Louisville: Westminster/John Knox Press, 1992.

Financial Planning:
Burkett, Larry. *Debt-Free Living*. Chicago, Illinois: Moody Press, 1989.

Career and Employment:
Bolles, Richard, N. *What Color Is Your Parachute?* Berkeley, CA: Ten Speed Press, 1996.

Burkett, Larry. *Business By The Book*. Nashville, TN: Thomas Nelson Publisher, 1990.

Ellis, Lee and Burkett, Larry. *Your Career In Changing Times*. Chicago, Ill: Moody Press, 1993.

Spiritual Warfare:
Frangipane, Francis. *The Three Battlegrounds*. Cedar Rapids, IA: Arrow Publications, 1989.

Murphy, Ed, Dr. *The Handbook for Spiritual Warfare*. Nashville, TN: Thomas Nelson Publisher, 1996.

Statistics, Studies, and Findings:
Surveys sent to clergy to assess responses to the problem of domestic violence.

Alsdurf, James and Phyllis. *Battered Into Submission*. Downers Grove, Illinois: Inter Varsity Press, 1989, p. 153. and "Wife Abuse and the Church: The Response of Pastors." Responses to the Victimization of Women and Children, 8/1: 9-11.

Johnson, John and Bondurant, Denise. "Revising the 1982 Church Response Survey," p. 422, a chapter in *Violence Against Women and Children*, editors Carol J. Adams and Marie M. Fortune, New York, NY: Continuum Publishing Co., 1995.

Video List on Domestic Violence

The following videos are given as a reference and do not necessarily represent the views of the author. Please call your state domestic violence coalition for more information. Many coalitions allow the public to borrow videos. Also, check with your local public library for videos on the subject of domestic violence.

Religious Community:
Broken Vows: Religious Perspectives on Domestic Violence
When You Preach...Remember Me
Confronting Sexism and Violence

Teen Dating Violence:
Friendship and Dating
My Girl: Battering in Teen Relationships
Rough Love

General Domestic Violence:
A Family Affair
Defending Our Lives
Escape the Abuse—Leaving Smart
Faces of Fear (PBS Documentary)
Rites of Violence
The Savage Cycle: Domestic Violence
Two Million Women
Violence in the Home: Living in Fear

Children And Domestic Violence:
Children of the Lie
It's Not Always Happy At My House
It's Not O.K., Let's Talk About Domestic Violence (ABA Commission)
You're Hurting Me, Too
Safe at Last (Teaching Guide)
Scenes from a Shelter (ages 2-7)
The Children are Watching
Secret Wounds

Special Populations:
About Love (Asian-American)
Dolores (Latino)
The Golden Years (Elder Abuse)
To Find Our Way and First Steps

(Native American)
Voices Heard—Sisters Unseen

Law Enforcement:
Police Response
The Law Enforcement Response:
Domestic Violence

Batterer's Intervention:
Ending Family Violence—for therapists, helpers, and counselors
The Truth About Domestic Violence—for offenders and families
Dynamics of Abuse
Choosing to End the Violence
The Savage Man

Resources for Teenagers

Books

Adams, Carol, et al. *No Is Not Enough: Helping Teenagers Avoid Sexual Assault.* San Luis Obispo, CA: Impact Pubs. Cal., 1984. Information about date rape.

Fortune, Marie M. *Sexual Abuse Prevention: A Study for Teenagers.* New York, NY: Pilgrim Press, 1984. Revised Edition, 1996. A five-session curriculum for twelve- to eighteen-year-olds, with a leader's guide to use with religious youth groups. To order call The Center for the Prevention of Sexual and Domestic Violence, (206) 634-1903.

Levy, Barrie. *Dating Violence: Young Women in Danger* and *In Love and Danger: A Teen's Guide to Breaking Free of Abusive Relationships.* Seattle, WA: Seal Press, 1991 and 1993, (206) 283-7844.

Sevig, Julie B., editor. *Beyond Violence: Empowering Youth to Make a Difference*, a retreat planning guide, 1997, by the Evangelical Lutheran Church in America. Call 1-800-638-3522, Ext. 2596.

Youngs, Sharon K. *Confronting Domestic Violence: Not Just For Adults.* Louisville: Presbyterian Publishing Corporation, 1996. A four-session curriculum for fourteen- to eighteen-year-olds; looks at the dynamics of violence and ways to confront it. Leader's Guide: $6.25. To order, call 1-800-227-2872.

Parenting for Peace and Justice Network: Print and audio-visual resources for families, congregations and schools; an international, interfaith network promoting family peacemaking, available from The Institute for Peace and Justice, 4144 Lindell Blvd., #408, St. Louis, MO 63108, (314) 533-4445.

Turn Off The Violence Program: for individuals and groups to educate people about non-violent entertainment and ways to deal with conflict. Write to Citizens Council, 822 South 3rd St., Suite 100, Minneapolis, MN 55415, (612) 348-6539.

Videos

Altschul Group, 1560 Sherman Ave., Suite 100, Evanston, IL 60201, 1-800-323-9084
"Crossing the Line: The Truth About Gangs" (18 minutes)
"Getting Along" (12 minutes)
"Weapons and You" (12 minutes)
Price: $295 each, $50 rental fee for five days

Coronet/MTI Film and Video, Washington Coalition of Sexual Abuse Programs, 110 E. Fifth Ave., Suite 214, Olympia, WA 98501, (360) 754-7583
"Scoring: Date Rape" (20 minutes) Price: $8 rental fee

Resources for Children

Print

White, Vera K. *The Family of God: Creating a Fair Community.* A five-session study for children in grades 3-6 on dealing with conflict and building community. Available from Presbyterian Distribution Service, 1-800-524-2612, #70-350-94-296.

Wilson, Faye. *A Call to Hope: Living as Christians in a Violent Society.* Includes a children's activity book and teacher's guide that helps children talk about violence; session one addresses the issue of domestic violence. Friendship Press Mission Study for Children, 1997-98.

Videos

"No punching Judy" (27 minutes), A five-week curriculum based on multigenerational religious education for the purpose of teaching skills children need to develop relationships free of violence. Video and curriculum available for sale and rental. Contact: Operations Department, Unitarian Universalist Service Committee, 130 Prospect St., Cambridge, MA 02139.

"Safe At Last", #7617-V, "Secret Wounds"—shows vignettes of children talking about family violence which may be used by counselors in individual or group therapy. Kidrights, 10100 Park Cedar Drive, Charlotte, NC 28210, 1-800-892-KIDS, Fax: (704) 541-0113.

Therapeutic Board Games

"Angry Animals", to teach problem-solving skills (ages 6-8 years).
"Breakaway", to teach healthy expressions of emotions (ages 9-12 years).
Kidsrights, 1-800-892-KIDS.

Internet Addresses

To research information about domestic violence, go to a search engine and type in the phrase "domestic violence" or "family violence." The following are web pages on the issue of domestic violence. The content is given for reference and does not necessarily represent the views of the author.

http://www.serve.com/ufc/facts.html
Childhelp USA National Statistics

http://www.s-t.com/projects/DomVio/conviction.html
Convictions

http://www.telalink.net:80/'police/abuse/#longterm
Dangers after separation

http://www.vicnet.net.au/%Ewise/DVContext.htm
Domestic violence

http://membersaol.com/SueMKent/DOVES.html
Domestic Violence Educational Services

http://www/cybergrrl.com/dv/book/myth.html
Facts and myths

http://www.fvpf.org/fund/
Family Violence Prevention Fund

http://www.volcanopress.com/tblcont.html
Family violence and religion

http://www.umn.edu/mincava/hart/legalro.htm
Legal road to freedom

http://www.webmerchants.com/ncadv
National Coalition Against Domestic Violence, Denver, CO

http://www.athens,net/~rblum/batpos.html
Men who batter

http://www.vix.com/men/battery/studies/pavenet.html
PAVNET: Partners Against Violence Network

http://www.vix.com/pub/men/battery/reconstruct.html
Reconstruction surgery for victims

http://www.pastornet.net.au:80/salvcamp/domviol2.htm
Statements from the Salvation Army

http://www.silcom.com/~paladin/madv/stats.html
Statistics from National Coalition Against Domestic Violence

http://www.abanet.org/cle/stopping.html
Stopping violence against women using federal laws

http://www.Now.org/issues/economic/welfref.html
Welfare reform & victims

http://www.cybergrrl.com/dv/ywca/ywca.html
YMCA information

Christian Recovery Addresses On The Internet

To research Christian recovery sites, go to a search engine and type in the phrase(s), Christian recovery/counseling/healing.

http://www.biblical-counseling.org/
Biblical Counseling Association

http://www.christians-in-recovery.com
Christians in recovery

http://hlom.org/index3.htm/
Healing Love Outreach Ministry

http://www.cris.com/~Herb/journey/
Journey Ministries

GLOSSARY

abuser—person who uses physical, emotional, verbal, sexual, spiritual, economic, or parental authority abuse to control another person.

antidepressant—a non-addictive medication used to treat some forms of diagnosed depression.

batterer—person who physically assaults spouse, children, partner, or family member with the intent to inflict pain.

battering—physically assaulting spouse, partner, children, or family member with the intent to inflict pain.

codependency—a state of being overly dependent upon a spouse or partner to the extent that it impairs normal functioning.

cognition/cognitive—refers to the thought process or thinking.

confession—speaking God's truth and acknowledging your own wrongness.

conscious—having awareness of thoughts and memories.

depression—an emotional mood disorder with the symptoms of sadness, crying, increased or decreased sleeping patterns, weight loss or gain, fatigue, and/or suicidal thoughts.

domestic violence shelter—a safe house supported and managed by a non-profit agency to provide temporary shelter and safety from batterers for women and children.

demoniac violence—the direct or indirect influence of the kingdom of evil in domestic violence situations.

generational domestic violence—any type of abuse learned in childhood and continued on into the next generation of family members.

generational curse—sin that is not dealt with in a family which therefore continues to manifest into other generations of the family, and even multiplies.

grace—a free gift from Jesus to show His love and mercy instead of condemnation.

Holy Spirit—the Spirit of God which resides in each Christian person.

Jehovah Rapha—a name for God in the Bible which means "God our Healer."

memory healing—processing and analyzing past thoughts about painful childhood events with the guidance of the Holy Spirit.

misogyny—conscious or subconscious hate and abuse by men of their spouses or partners; religious misogynists are religious men who hate their spouses/girlfriends.

narcissistic—refers to a self-centered, egotistical, selfish person.

pathological—a habitual pattern of compulsive behavior.

post traumatic stress disorder—emotional illness caused by a tragic and painful event in the past.

redemption—the act of Jesus when He shed His blood to save humanity from spiritual death.

repentance—being sorry for a sin and permanently stopping the sin.

restitution—when a person rights the wrongs he/she has caused to another person.

resurrection—refers to Jesus when He arose on the third day after He was crucified on the cross.

repressed memories—memories that are pressed down into the unconscious mind so the person cannot remember them, but which still influence the person's thoughts and behaviors.

saved—refers to salvation, accepting, believing, and confessing Jesus Christ as your Lord and Savior.

stronghold—a human weakness that Satan uses to tempt a person into habitual sinful behaviors.

subconscious—not having a full awareness of one or more past memories about a painful childhood event.

support/treatment/education group for male batterers—a weekly therapy group for male abusers lead by a male mental health professional. A Christian group is lead by a male Christian counselor and/or minister. A femal therapist can be a co-leader.

suppressed memories—pushing the conscious painful memories aside and not thinking about them.

transitional house—a house supported by a nonprofit agency for the male batterers to stay in until counseling is completed and the physical abuse has stopped permanently. Batterers may continue to work to financially support their families.

unconscious—not having any awareness of one or more past painful childhood events.

End Notes

Introduction:
1. Schwartz, Karen,. "Till Death Do Us Part:" The hidden secret of marital violence, *Herald of Holiness*, (1995), p. 34.
2. Report to the Nations on Crime and Justice, Bureau of Justice Statistics, 1983.

Chapter One: Types of Abuse
1. Susan Reed, Fannie Weinstein, and Vickie Bane. The Kindest Cut, *People*, (4-22-96) pp. 67-70.
2. Lela Johnson, *The Beautiful Side of Submission*, (North Brunswick, NJ: Bridge-Logos, 1996), p. 1.
3. Dr. Bobby Miller, New Hope Counseling Manual, Line from poem: Secrets, (Huntington, WV: Copyright, 1991)
4. Uniform Crime Reports, Federal Bureau of Investigation, 1990.
5. Ross County Family Violence Council Pamphlet, 1995.
6. Westchester County Business Journal, Vol. 35, 08-05-1996, p. 13.
7. National Victims Center, Employee Liability for Workplace Violence, 1996.
8. National Coalition Against Domestic Violence Brochure, Denver, Co.
9. U.S. Attorney General's Task Force on Family Violence, September, 1984.

Chapter Two: Crisis Intervention
1. Davidson, T. (1977) Wife Beating: A Recurring phenomenon Throughout History. In Maria Roy (Ed.), Battered Women: A Psychological Study of Domestic Violence, New York: Nostrand Reinhold.
2. Finn, P. and Colson, S. (1996). Civil Protection Orders: Legislation, Current Court Practice, and Enforcement. Issues and Practice in Criminal Justice. Washington, DC: National Institute of Justice.
3. Hart, B. (1996). Gentle Jeopardy, *Mediation Quarterly*, 7:4, p. 324.
4. Hart, B. (1991). Safety Planning for Children: Strategy for Unsupervised Visits with Batterers. Battering and Addiction: Consciousness-Raising for Battered Women and Advocates. Harrisburg, PA: PCADV.
5. National Coalition Against Domestic Violence Pamphlet, Denver, Co.
6. Davis, Robert C. and Smith, Barbara, "Domestic Violence Reforms: Empty Promises or Fulfilled Expectations?", *Crime and Delinquency*, 41. n4, (1995) p. 541-552.
7. Jackson, James G., "Ending the Cycle of Domestic Violence, *The Police Chief*, V63, n2, (Feb. 1996), p 33.
8. National Clearinghouse on Families and Youth, Silver Springs, MD., Feb. 21, 1996.
9. Ohio Children's Trust Fund: A Guide for Mandated Reporters, Child Abuse and Neglect, Ross County Children's Services, Chillicothe, Ohio, 1996.
10. Elizabeth Schneider, Legal Reform for Battered Women, 1990.
11. Ohio Domestic Violence Network Pamphlet, Columbus, Ohio, 1997.

12. Senate Judiciary Committee Hearings, 1990.
13. U.S. Dept. of Justice, 1993.
14. U.S. Commission on Civil Rights, 1982.
15. Attorney General's Family Violence Task Force of Pennsylvania, 1989.
16. Action Ohio Coalition for Battered Women Manual, Columbus, Ohio, 1997.

Chapter Three: Christian Men Who Batter
1. Diagnostic and Statistical Manual of Mental Disorders, (DSM-IV), American Psychological Association, Washington, DC.
2. Rinck, Dr. Margaret J., *Christian Men Who Hate Women*, (Grand Rapids, Michigan: Zondervan, 1990).
3. Smolowe, Jill, "When Violence Hits Home", *Time*, (July 4, 1994), p. 22.
4. For Shelter and Beyond, Massachusetts Coalition of Battered Women Service Groups, Boston, MA, 1990.

Chapter Four: Women, Men, and the Bible
1. Alsdurf, Phyllis and James, *Battered Into Submission*, Downers Grove, Illinois: InterVarsity Press, 1989, p. 11.
2. Kroger, Catherine Clark, a chapter entitled, "Let's Look at the Biblical Concept of Submission," in *Violence Against Women and Children*, p.135.

Chapter Five: Jesus Therapy
1. Smolowe, Jill, "When Violence Hits Home", *Time*, (July 4, 1994), p. 22.
2. Strong, James, *Strong's Exhaustive Concordance of The Bible*, (Nashville, TN: Thomas Nelson Publishers, 1990), p. 164.
3. Murphy, Dr. Ed, *The Handbook for Spiritual Warfare*, Nashville, TN: Thomas Nelson Publisher, 1996, p. 463.
4. Duewel, Wesley L., *Mighty Prevailing Prayer*, Grand Rapids, Michigan: Zondervan Publishing House, 1990, p. 15 and p. 266.
5. Frangipane, Francis, *The Three Battlegrounds*, Cedar Rapids, IA: Arrow Publications, 1989, p. 86.
6. References: Chemical People Newsletter.

Chapter Six: Batterer to Believer
1. Sanford, John and Paula, *Transformation of the Inner Man*, South Plainfield, NJ: Bride Publishing, 1982, p. 11.
2. Littauer, Fred, *Promise of Restoration*, San Bernardino, CA: Here's Life Publisher, 1990, p. 50.

Chapter Seven: Victim to Victor
1. Block, Carolyn, Illinois Criminal Justice Information, Newsweek (July 4, 1994), p. 33.
2. Walker, Lenore E.A., "Legal Self-Defense Issues for Women of Color," Unpublished paper, 1988.
3. National Coalition Against Domestic Violence Voice Newsletter, Winter 1989.

4. BJS Executive Summary: Spouse Murder Defendants in Large Urban Counties (NCJ-156831), September 1995, p.1.
5. BJS Selected Findings: Violence Between Intimates, (NCJ-149259), November 1994, p. 2.
6. Littauer, Fred, *The Promise of Restoration*, San Bernardino, CA: Here's Life Publisher, 1990, p. 86.
7. Frank, Jan and Don, *When Victims Marry Victims*, San Bernardino, CA: Here's Life Publisher, 1990, p. 32.
8. Hart, Barbara, National Violence, 1988.
9. Uniform Crime Reports, Federal Bureau of Investigation, 1991.

Chapter Eight: Trauma to Triumph
1. Roy, Maria, *Children in the Crossfire*, NCADV Fact Sheet, 1988.
2. Russell, Diana, 1986, Childhelp USA National Statistics, 1996.
3. National Coalition Against Domestic Violence Fact Sheet, Denver, Co.
4. Levy, Dating Violence: Young Women in Danger, 1991.
5. Roscoe, B. and Callahan. J., "Adolescent's Self-Report of Violence in Families and Dating Relationships," *Adolescence*, Vol. XX, No. 79, Fall 1985.
6. National Coalition Against Domestic Violence Fact Sheet, Denver, Co.
7. The American Academy of Pediatrics.

Chapter Nine: Hurting to Hope
1. Roy, Maria, *Children in the Crossfire*, NCADV Fact Sheet, 1988.
2. Walker, Lenore, *The Battered Woman Syndrome*, 1984.
3. Pfout, Schopler, & Henley, "Forgotten Victims of Family Violence," *Social Work*, July 1982.
4. Jaffe, Wolfe, & Wilson, *Children of Battered Women*, 1990.
5. Ohio Children's Trustfund, Child Abuse, & Neglect: A Guide for Mandated Reporters.
6. National Coalition Against Domestic Violence Fact Sheet, Denver, Co.
7. Child Advocate, Fall 1994.
8. March of Dimes, 1992.
9. Action Ohio Coalition for Battered Women Manual, Columbus, Ohio, 1997.

Chapter Ten: Marital Restoration
1. Swindoll, Chuck, *Strike the Original Match*, (Portland, OR: Mutnomah, 1980).

Chapter Thirteen: Tools for Counseling
1. Nee, Watchman, *The Spiritual Man*, (New York, NY: Christian Fellowship Publishers, 1968). V.11, Part Four, p. 7.
2. Ibid., Part Five, p. 158.

Review of Chapters

CHAPTER 1, Types of abuse
    Definition of domestic violence
    Physical
    Emotional/psychological
    Spiritual
    Verbal
    Sexual
    Social
    Economical/financial
    Parental authority
    Wives being murdered by husbands
    Abuse of children and teenagers
    Vignette

CHAPTER 2, Crisis Intervention
    Safety plan for victims/children
    How did Jesus handle a crisis?
    Scenarios
    Assessment of crisis situation
    Pastors, how can you help?
    Hostage situations
    Child abuse assessment
    Why do women stay?
    Suicide assessment
    Homicide assessment
    Police intervention, state and federal laws
    Vignette

CHAPTER 3, Christian Men who Batter
    Are batterers Christians?
    Characteristics of a batterer
    Misogyny
    Types of men who batter
    Vignette

CHAPTER 4, Women, Men, and the Bible
    Roles of women
    The meaning of the word submission
    Value of women to Jesus
    Scriptures men use to justify abuse
    Importance of Bible study in interpretation
    Vignette

CHAPTER 5, Jesus Therapy
    Causes of domestic violence
    Denial and blame
    Deception, sin, and rebellion
    Learned family violence
    Generational curses, demons, and strongholds
    Wrong thinking
    A weak conscience

Review of Chapters

    Appetite for power and control
    Emotions out of balance
    Violent anger
    Inability to love and pathological jelousy
    Childhood sexual abuse
    Addiction to pornography
    Inaccurate view of God as Father
    Alcohol and drug abuse
    Unforgiveness
    Stress
    Low to no self-concept
    Lack of social skills
    Mental disorders
    Guild and shame
    Fear of abandonment
    Unsubmissive to God
    Unhealthy boundaries
    Selfishness and pride
    Sense of meaningless and despair
    Domestic/demoniac violence
    Church discipline
    Vignette

CHAPTER 6, Batterer to Believer
    12 Step Christian Recovery Program
    Denail system of batteres
    Support/Treatment/Education groups
    Daily formula
    Spiritual inventory
    Anger activity
    ABC's
    Cycle of violence
    Vignette

CHAPTER 7, Victim to Victor
    Devotions
    Treatment
    Questionnaire
    African American women
    Victims and healing
    Codependency
    Victim/victor language
    Daily formula
    12 Step Christian Recovery Program
    Vignette

CHAPTER 8, Trauma to Triumph
    12 Step Christian Recovery Program for teenagers
    Treatment
    Suicide intervention
    No suicide contract
    Dating violence
    Vignette

CHAPTER 9, Hurting to Hope
- 12 Step Christian Recovery Program for children
- Treatment
- Signs of child abuse
- Casualties of war
- Unborn casualties of war
- Vignette

CHAPTER 10, Marital Restoration
- Guidelines
- Goals and treatment for restoration
- Counseling sessions
- Communication skills
- Conflict resolution
- Putting God in the marriage
- Divorce and separation
- Vignette
- Family restoration
- Family counseling
- How parents can help adult children who are victims
- Vignette

CHAPTER 11, Prevention of Domestic Violence
- How can the church help?
- Married adults, singles, teenager
- What can the Christian community do?
- How can pastors help?
- How can secular and religious communities work together?
- Scripture for battered women
- How can parents and friends help?

CHAPTER 12, Poetry Therapy
- Poetry
- Poems and stories

CHAPTER 13, Tools for Counseling
- Holy Spirit
- Balance wheel
- Anger management contract
- Anger Factory
- Thought Stopping Maps and Behavior Chains
- Genographs
- Scriptures for renewing of mind
- Mirror exercise
- Self-talk

INDEX

Abandonment, 82, 95
Abortion, 150
Abuse, 11
Accountability, 104
Addiction, 88
Adolescence, 134
Adultery, 16
AIDS, 128, 135
Alcohol, 88, 138
Anger, 80, 109, 136, 189, 191-195
Assessment, 25, 139
Behavior, 196
Bible, 59, 65, 153
Blame, 70
Boundaries, 96
Child Abuse, 34
Children, 18, 145
Christian shelter, 28
Church, 101
Civil protection order, 47
Coalitions, 211
Codependency, 123
Confidentiality, 29
Control, 64, 77
Crime, 47
Crisis, 21
Dating, 139
Deliverance, 100
Demons, 74
Denial, 70, 105
Depression, 128
Devotions, 115
Divorce, 161
Domestic violence, 11, 70
Drugs, 88
DSM - IV, 54
Economic abuse, 17
Emotion, 78
Emotional abuse, 13

Families, 163
Fasting, 80
Father, 87, 164
Fear, 70, 82
Federal Law, 43
Felony, 48
Forgiveness, 84, 90
Generational curses, 74
Genograph, 197-200
Guilt, 94
Head Trauma, 55
Healing, 108, 122
Holy Spirit, 123, 187
Homicide, 41
Hostage, 30
Hotlines, 207-210
Internet, 235
Intervention, 22
Intimacy, 160
Jealousy, 85
Love, 85
Marital rape, 16
Marriage, 102, 119, 156, 174
Meaninglessness, 99
Medical, 26, 128
Memory, 86
Mental disorders, 93
Military, 54, 58, 94
Mind, 201
Misogynies, 53
Narcissistic, 94
Neglect, 35.
Ohio laws, 45
Parental authority abuse, 17
Parents, 173
Pastors, 28, 54, 57
Physical abuse, 12, 147
Poems, 176
Police, 25

Pornography, 87
Power, 77
Prayer, 100, 159
Prevention, 140, 167
Pride, 97
Prison, 82
Protection order, 47
P.T.S.D., 93
Rebellion, 74
Reconciliation, 156
Repentant, 91
Restoration, 155
Satan, 69, 100
Safety, 31, 33
Self - control, 80
Self - esteem, 92
Self - talk, 75, 204
Sexual abuse, 16, 86, 148
Shame, 94
Shelters, 27, 171
Sin, 82
Social abuse, 16
Spiritual abuse, 14
Spiritual warfare, 71, 74
Stalking, 46
Step-families, 135
Stress, 91
Strongholds, 69
Submission, 14, 61
Suicide, 39, 138, 142
Support groups, 103
Surgery, 13
Teenagers, 143, 167
Television, 141
Therapy, 69, 104
Triggers, 82
Truth, 71
Verbal abuse, 15
Victims, 115, 118, 121, 126
Videos, 231
Weapons, 27
Welfare, 184

The ABC's of Salvation

A. <u>Admit</u> you have sinned.
"If we say that we have no sin, we deceive ourselves,
and the truth is not in us."
(1 John 1:8)

B. <u>Believe</u> in the Savior, Jesus Christ.
"For God so loved the world, that He gave his only
begotten Son, that whosoever believes in Him should
not perish, but have everlasting life."
(John 3:16)

C. <u>Confess</u> and forsake your sin.
"If we confess our sins, He is faithful and just to forgive
us our sins, and to cleanse us from all unrighteousness."
(1 John 1:9)

The ABC's of Rededication

A. <u>Ask</u> for forgiveness: confess and repent before God.
"Those whom I love, I reprove and discipline; be
zealous therefore, and repent."
(Revelation 3:19)

B. <u>Break</u> the bondage of Satan by the power of the blood of Jesus.
"Submit therefore to God. Resist the devil and
he will flee from you."
(James 4:7)

C. <u>Commit</u> yourself to Jesus Christ, prayer, and Bible reading
"He has told you, O man, what is good; And what does
the Lord require of you but to do justice, to love
kindness, And to walk humbly with your God?"
(Micah 6:8)

Order Form

Postal orders:
Melissa Martin, P.O. Box 61, Circleville, OH 43113

Telephone orders: (740) 477-6850

Please send *For Better or For Worse: A Blessing or A Curse?* **to**:

Name:_____

Address:_____

City:_____ State:_____

Zip:_____

Telephone: (_____) _____

Book Price: $15.00 in U.S. dollars.

Shipping: $4.00 for the first book and $1.00 for each additional book to cover shipping and handling within US, Canada, and Mexico. International orders add $7.00 for the first book and $3.00 for each additional book.

Feedback, Please

Feedback from victims, survivors, batterers, counselors, pastors, and helpers is essential for future editions. Write or e-mail your stories, experiences, comments, and recommendations to:

P.O. Box 61
Circleville, OH 43113
or
e-mail: martin@dragonbbs.com